Gender, Lies and Suicide

A WHISTLEBLOWER SPEAKS OUT

Walt Heyer

GENDER, LIES AND SUICIDE
Copyright © 2013 by Walt Heyer

ISBN: 978-1492100737

Dedication

To the lives that have been lost to suicide and
to their friends and loved ones who wonder
"What could I have done?"

That pain runs deep.

Foreword

From the dedication written by my friend and counselor, Dr. Dennis Gurnsey, in the front cover of my Bible so many years ago—

Walt,

How long the journey, How twisted the road. How tired you've been at times, weary, discouraged beyond description. But how faithful has God been through it all. I am deeply appreciative of the power of God's grace in your life and the special place those people we both love have forever in your life.

It's still day by day.

Your friend in Christ
Dennis L. Gurnsey
August 1985

Table of Contents

Introduction

Perhaps you are about to read for the first time testimonies of regret and evidence of suicide deaths for people who suffer gender distress. It takes courage for a whistle blower from inside the community to speak out publically about the massive failure of the current diagnostic approach and treatment for people with gender issues. That whistle blower is me—a maverick among transgenders, a male surgically altered to female who lived eight years as Laura Jensen, now happily living in my original birth gender.

At first I thought I was the only transgender who had regret or almost committed suicide. Now thirty years after my life-altering surgery I realize I'm just one in a population of silent, shame-filled individuals who suffer from a needless gender change. Yet, for all the pain, we are the lucky ones because at least we did not take our own lives. The cries from dark graves sound deafeningly in my ears, begging for someone to listen and help stop the madness that resulted in their deaths.

Watching one-sided media interviews which glorify happy outcomes using half truths and even outright false information over the years became way too much for me to stomach. The time has arrived to expose the various power groups, those shrill voices which drown out or destroy anything and anyone who does not go along with their overarching stratagem.

As you will see in this book, 41% of transgenders surveyed say they had attempted suicide at some point, and a much higher proportional of transgenders commit suicide than in the general population. I believe two major factors drive this tragedy.

First, the blind spots in the treatment protocol are so big you could drive a truck through them. The pre-transition treatment protocol (aka, the Standards of Care) does not require in-depth evaluation for depression or stressors that could be driving the compulsive desire to change genders.

Second, a strictly medical issue has been hijacked for ideological purposes. Activists use the alarming statistics of transgender suicide to blame society and to demand new transgender freedom laws.

The two factors are intertwined, conspiring to make sure you do not learn the truth.

Here's the truth: changing genders is suicide.

In case you do not think this book is vitally important for the transgender community, read this note from a man who wrote to me recently. His life mirrors the state of my life 30 years ago. He followed the protocol for getting surgery over the proper time period and got the two required letters of approval but surgery was not effective and his regret is making him suicidal.

Walt, I hope you can help me.

I'm in my 40s, a little more than one year after my sex change surgery, male to female. I struggled with my gender identity for most of my life. Because of my sex change surgery I'm miserable every day. It is so difficult every minute. I pray for the strength not to go to the gun store. I'm filled with suicidal thoughts because of my gender change surgery. I can't live like this anymore. Please help me. Guide me what to do medically, surgically

I caused this "bad dream." I have no one to blame but myself for getting so lost in a sick, destructive, obsessed fetish that drove me to such lengths that I so mistakenly thought SRS [sex reassignment surgery] was the solution. That's the problem I have with myself. I want to lock myself up for having been so delusional.

Now I'm half of a man. It's tragic. And no one in the medical field tried to stop me. It's a sick industry that needs to be stopped. You can get SRS almost as easy as buying a pack of chewing gum. It's absurd. And you are so right; it did not change my gender. It turned me into a nothing. Devoid of any pleasure or life. Why? Please tell me how I could have gotten so lost? Please explain that for me, Walt? Please help me to understand myself? I can't even figure out how I got here. I supposedly have some intelligence. I'm truly sick.

This man on the brink of suicide sought me out after finding and reading my website, sexchangeregret.com. He came to me already certain that a return to his birth gender is the only way to restore his sanity. I was able to comfort him with the knowledge that I'm here. I made it back from the edge of the same abyss he faces and I will do what I can to support him in his journey.

Various surveys and studies presented in this book show that a staggering number of gender changers will think about or commit suicide both before and after surgery. The goal of this book is to provide a fresh prospective on why this is so.

41% Attempt Suicide

1

In a national survey of 6,500 transgenders the question was
asked: "Have you ever attempted suicide?"
41% answered yes.[1]

Several months after my surgery I became extremely depressed. Life looked hopeless; my thoughts turned to suicide when I discovered the gender surgery may have been unnecessary.

The transgender suicide rates are not of my fabrication. The information is abundant but ignored.

---

[1] Jaime M. Grant, Ph.D., Lisa A. Mottet, J.D., and Justin Tanis, D.Min. With Jody L. Herman, Ph.D., Jack Harrison, and Mara Keisling, "National Transgender Discrimination Survey Report on health and health care / Findings of a Study by the National Center for Transgender Equality and the National Gay and Lesbian Task Force," October 2010, downloaded on March 23, 2011 from http://www.thetaskforce.org/downloads/reports/reports/ ntds_report_on_health.pdf

A study published in *Metabolism* states: "The number of deaths in male-to-female transsexuals was five times the number expected, due to increased numbers of suicide and death of unknown cause." [2]

A long-term follow-up (over 30 years) of 324 transsexual persons undergoing sex reassignment surgery in Sweden reported that surgically sex-reassigned persons have considerably higher risks for mortality and suicidal behavior.[3]

An international review of studies that followed over 2,000 persons in 13 countries who had undergone gender reassignment surgery identified 16 possible suicide deaths which, if confirmed, translates to a rate of suicide that is seven times the national average.[4]

Web sites that specialize in transgender suicide prevention report an alarmingly high rate of transgender

---

[2] Asscheman H, Gooren LJ, Eklund PL., "Mortality and morbidity in transsexual patients with cross-gender hormone treatment", *Metabolism*. 1989 Sep; 38(9):869-73. Downloaded on May 17, 2013 from http://www.ncbi.nlm.nih.gov/pubmed/2528051

[3] Dhejne C, Lichtenstein P, et. al., "Long-Term Follow-Up of Transsexual Persons Undergoing Sex Reassignment Surgery: Cohort Study in Sweden", op. cit.

[4] "Suicide and Suicide Risk in Lesbian, Gay, Bisexual, and Transgender Populations: Review and Recommendations", Ann P. Haas, Mickey Eliason, et. al., *Journal of Homosexuality*, Vol. 58, Issue 1, 2010, downloaded on June 14, 2013, from http://www.ncbi.nlm.nih.gov/pmc/articles/PMC3662085/

suicide and suicide attempts, some estimate as high as 50%.[5] This is a clear message that the surgical change is not very effective in treating the gender distressed.

Perhaps you think, as I did, with all the new laws being pushed through by activists, schools and medical practitioners, and easy access to surgeons specializing in the transgender surgery, all transgenders are happy; you're wrong, even dead wrong.

At some point in their lives before, during, or even after taking the path to gender change, over 40% will become so distraught and depressed they will attempt suicide and unfortunately, many will die.

We have a perfect setup for the great "con": the suffering patients, who are clearly in need of relief and will do most anything to get it, and the charlatans who prey on them to further their own agenda, whether it is political, prestige or simple greed.

The entire co-dependent gender change community— the physicians, psychologists and surgeons who make their living from the transgender population and the activists who have a political agenda—need to be held accountable. They are responsible, either directly or indirectly, by turning a blind eye to the suicide rate and what may be causing it.

The staggering numbers have not even slightly lifted the eyebrows of the media. It seems that in the social war against traditional marriage and to normalize non-conforming genders,

---

[5] Lauras-Playground.com, "Transgender, Transsexual, Peers Wanted for Suicide Prevention Help," Downloaded February 1, 2011 from http://www.lauras-playground.com/transgender_peers_suicide.htm

transgenders are the hidden casualties, almost one-third of them sacrificed for the higher cause. One of my desires is to apply pressure on the media, getting them to consider the important role they can play in saving lives from unfortunate suicide by shining a light on the hidden carnage.

Something causes people to commit suicide or attempt it. Suicide is a widely-studied field of research. I'm hoping the ideas in this book will open a window of fresh thinking about the links between transgenders and suicides.

On a side note—I want to distinguish between the heterosexual who suffers from gender dysphoria and the homosexual who has other reasons for a gender change. Homosexuals, no doubt, also suffer from the same psychological and psychiatric disorders, but the focus in this book will be solely on the heterosexual transgender with disabling gender issues.

Even transgenders who supposedly "have it all" commit suicide. In Toronto, a prominent and much-loved transgender activist named Kyle Scanlon committed suicide in 2012, as reported by advocate.com:

> *Toronto Mourns Suicide of Transgender Leader*
> by Diane Anderson-Minshall, July 11, 2012
> Toronto residents are grieving the loss of transgender activist Kyle Scanlon, who the Torontoist called "a valued leader, gifted mentor, and much-loved friend" after Scanlon took his own life July 3... Toronto's Trans PULSE project (which Scanlon helped found)... reminded readers that 'depression, hopelessness and

suicide are very real issues for trans people and Kyle's death has and will continue to hit the community very hard.'"[6]

We do not know the story behind this tragedy, but the article clearly says that Scanlon was much loved and his death prompted Toronto's Trans PULSE project, a group he helped start, to remind readers of the risks brought about by changing genders—*depression, hopelessness and suicide*—a transgender plague.

In the U.S., the Transgender Task Force, a leading advocate group for non-conforming genders and transgenders, conducted a survey of transgenders. In the published results, *Injustice at Every Turn*, the group reports that a large proportion of transgenders will attempt suicide: "A staggering 41% reported attempting suicide." [7]

But wait, you say. Everything I have read or watched on TV portrays the overwhelming success of sex changes. You probably have the same impression I do: transgenders are all so happy that they changed genders; no regrets. In this book, I want to explore the discrepancy between the success reported in the media and the conclusions of certain research studies. I want to look behind the smiles at the hidden sign of failure, that is, the high rate of suicides.

---

[6] Diane Anderson-Minshall, *Toronto Mourns Suicide of Transgender Leader*, Advocate.com, July 11, 2012, downloaded from http://www.advocate.com/ politics/transgender/2012/07/11/toronto-mourns-suicide-transgender-leader

[7] Grant, Jaime M., et. al., *Injustice at Every Turn: A Report of the National Transgender Discrimination Survey.* op. cit.

This search for answers reminds me of the carnival worker standing in the arcade with 3 shells on a flat board, one shell hiding a little pea. "Which one hides the pea?" he asks as he shuffles the shells. We will need to look under many shells to find the truths hidden in the case of transgender suicide.

Let's begin with what we can learn from the onset of gender distress.

Dysphoria Is a Disorder

2

"I AM a non-person, an 'it'. I have let them mutilate me. Far from solving my problems, the operation has made things worse."

Sandra, formerly Peter, had a sex-change operation in 1987, when she was 40. At the time of the operation she was having panic attacks and was heavily dependent on tranquillizers. Now she is finally coming off them, an alarming certainty is dawning on her: the surgery should never have taken place.

"I had a very unhappy childhood. My father was violent, and by the time I was in my twenties my doctor was prescribing high doses of tranquillizers. I tried to lead a normal life. I got

married and even thought about having children,
but the panic attacks kept coming at me."[8]

To help people with gender issues we need to better understand them and the onset of their distress. My own mother admitted only months prior to her death that her early discipline once was so severe she thought she had killed me. Throughout my childhood, she told me I was different. Her often repeated opinion of me became my reality and may have contributed to my mental disorders and transgenderism.

In the mental health field, the tool most widely referenced by clinicians is the Diagnostic and Statistical Manual of Mental Disorders (DSM), published since 1952 by The American Psychiatric Association and now in its fifth revision. The latest updates sparked much controversy, but after much committee work and discussion, gender identity disorder has been renamed with a softer term, gender dysphoria.

I looked up the meaning of the term dysphoria and the definition definitely caught my attention. Dysphoria is "an emotional state characterized by anxiety, depression, or unease."[9] So we see transgenders diagnosed with gender dysphoria do suffer from anxiety and depression. So while the activists blame society and its discrimination and abuse for

---

[8] Lonsdale, Sarah, "When sex-change is a mistake: Some transsexuals suffer bitter regrets.", Sunday 24 October 1993, *The Independent*, http://www.independent.co.uk/life-style/when-sexchange-is-a-mistake-some-transsexuals-suffer-bitter-regrets-sarah-lonsdale-reports-1512822.html

[9] http://www.thefreedictionary.com/dysphoria

transgender suicide, they are reluctant to address the depression that often starts early.

Family is ground zero for the onset of depression. We can look back at a person's early childhood and discover where the gender depression seed was planted and started to grow. The evolution of a transgender is slow. It is begun and reinforced by lost relationships, unhealthy relationships, or interactions that foster the desire to change genders. Physical and sexual abuse and family breakups and other dynamics all become factors in the psychological development of gender expression.

Gender dysphoria relates to stress and discomfort caused by a perceived discrepancy between self identified gender and assigned gender at birth. [10]

I do not blame transgenders for the way they express the discomfort they have regarding their sense of self. But as one surgeon from Portugal put it, just because someone says they are Napoleon doesn't mean the medical community should agree.[11] The collaborative medical community is contributing to eventual suicide by refusing to consider the long term

---

[10] WPATH Standards of Care (World Professional Association for Transgender Health), "Standards of Care for the Health of Transsexual, Transgender, and Gender Nonconforming People", 7th Version, 2011, downloaded from http://www.wpath.org/documents/ Standards%20of%20Care%20V7%20-%202011%20WPATH.pdf, p. 7

[11] Inês Raposo, "WALT HEYER: Mudar de corpo e voltar" *PÚBLICO*, 30.11.2012, http://lifestyle.publico.pt/artigos/313679_mudar-de-corpo-e-voltar (downloaded March 5, 2013)

consequences of giving hormone blockers to pre-pubescent children and cross-gender hormone injections and surgery to the mentally distressed. It is madness.

Not everyone with this diagnosis will dive into the full regimen of cross-gender hormones but I did for many years. My surgeon, Dr. Stanley Biber, had performed 1,000 or so of the surgeries by the time I landed on his operating table in Trinidad, Colorado, in April of 1983. He documented in an affidavit that the surgical procedure had changed me from Walt Heyer, male, to Laura Jensen, female. To show you how mentally unstable I was, when I entered the hospital for gender surgery I signed the papers using the name Andrea West even though my legal name was Walt Heyer. But immediately after surgery I called myself Laura Jensen.

A longtime friend, Marcella, shares her personal thoughts and observations in the time leading up to the surgery and in the days afterwards as I stayed with her to recover:

Full of anxiety, I waited to hear from the new Laura. Though happy for Walt, because he convinced me the surgery was absolutely necessary for his happiness, I had my secret doubts. In hindsight, I wonder if I should have mentioned my reservations. Dressing up as a woman, putting on nail polish and make-up was a fun aspect of his need to feel like a woman, but such radical surgery is serious business. I did nothing to dissuade him. I respected Walt's decision on becoming Laura, and I was committed to supporting a very dear friend.

I witnessed Walt's constant struggle to resolve a life long desire to become a female. The breast implants, electrolysis for facial hair removal, Adam's apple reduction, fanny lift surgery, all the agonizing pain seemed to be worth it to him. His love of alcohol helped him guide the way.

I knew Walt (as Andrea) obtained a surgical approval letter from Dr. Paul Walker who attested he was in stable mental health. We both laughed about the approval letter, thinking it was cool that he saved tons of time and money by getting the letter so quickly. How foolish we were. Anyway, that's all Walt needed, a green light, no caution light flashing here.

Walt went in for surgery as a male and came out as Laura Jensen, female. It was amazing to me that such a thing was possible, and supposedly life would be much better than before, at least that was the plan. He explained the procedure to me. I understood it. I thought he was very brave.

Laura finally arrived at my home from his flight from Colorado where the surgery took place. He looked fine but tired. He told me the doctors stressed for him to follow the post-surgery procedures.

I had to get used to having a new girlfriend. Laura acted like a woman, but I could still see my old friend Walt through all the changes. I loved them both. We giggled like school girls. The same hilarious sense of humor Walt had existed in Laura.

One night we went to a club for a few drinks and dancing. Watching Laura getting asked to dance more than I did taxed my confidence, but I was happy for her. It all seemed so right for awhile. But things changed.

"I never should have had the surgery," Laura said one day. "It was a mistake."

"Aha," I said, "There is a good reason for a true psychiatric evaluation." It was too late for Walt, at least for a complete reversal.

I wanted you to see Marcella's firsthand account of my early days because it tells the same old story repeated by countless transgenders over the years. The transgender convinces everyone around him surgery is necessary. Approval is easy and quick. Great excitement leads up to the new gender. But eight years later: full blown regret and an "about face" to restore the life that was lost.

I lived with some success as a female for eight years, but I remained psychologically depressed with persistent unease about who I was. Having the surgery did not stop the depression. In fact, thoughts of suicide intensified because of my long-term struggle with my gender identity.

The long-term Swedish study mentioned in Chapter 1 that found persons with transsexualism, after sex reassignment, have considerably higher risk for mortality, suicidal behavior and psychiatric morbidity coincides with my own struggle with suicide. This has elevated my concern about others who are suffering as I did. Writing this book is my attempt to wave a caution flag, to start a dialogue and to help prevent suicides. I know the hard truth is distressing, but someone needs raise awareness about transgender suicide, not using it as an excuse to indict society for not being accepting enough, but to expand the discussion and allow transgenders to get evaluated and treated.

Studies that show the link between suicides and comorbid (a medical term meaning "coexisting") disorders are not difficult to find; it is typically hard to find media willing to talk about the suicides among transgenders without spinning the story to promote the advocates' agenda.

Now you have the opportunity to hear the inside story from a person with a unique point-of-view—a whistleblower who has lived in the transgender community.

Dr. Money,
a Reckless Narcissist

3

The original 1979 standards became the means for justifying
sex change surgery on demand.

In the later years of the 1970s, the American Psychiatric
Association was preparing the third revision of its flagship
manual, DSM-III (Diagnostic and Statistical Manual of Mental
Disorders, Version 3). In it, the diagnosis for transgenders was
going to be Gender Identity Disorder or GID.

The DSM-III identified the family environment during
childhood development—the interaction and influence of mom
and dad, siblings, extended family, caregivers—as a cause of
Gender Identity Disorders. The DSM also pointed to the lack of
effective gender-role reinforcement from the mom or dad as a
factor in the onset of gender disorders. In other words, the
parents, family and environment highly influence a child's

gender development. What you will not see in the DSM-III is any of the false information suggesting that hormone brain wash or brain abnormality is the factor.[12] (Those misleading theories, by the way, have been disproved over the years.)

Dr. Money, the sexologist, and Dr. Walker, the social psychologist, were promoting gender surgery and the idea that gender could be changed and artificially fashioned by surgery. They were not about to embrace the American Psychiatric Association causal factors nor were they going to accept a diagnosis that included the word disorder. They were aware that the DSM would promote psychotherapy as the recommended treatment for the psychological condition called GID, not surgery. The logical outcome would be the marginalization of sex change surgery.

Money and his reputation were about to take a hit at his home base, Johns Hopkins Hospital. After twelve years of asserting gender was learned and backing it up with falsified research results, Money found himself on the losing side. Results from a 1978 follow-up study of the patients treated at Hopkins were being gathered. They showed no improvement from surgery, reinforcing the view that gender issues were psychologically based and surgery was not helpful. That study would lead to the end of sex change surgery at Hopkins.

From all I can tell, the closing of the clinic and the release of the DSM-III was a double whammy of bad transgender news. I feel it had the potential to stop future gender surgeries and it prompted Dr. Money, Dr. Walker and Dr. Harry Benjamin to

---

[12] DSM-III-R, page 73

work quickly to cobble together a group of like-minded surgical activists to draft standards of care exclusively for transgenders ahead of the 1980 release of the DSM-III.

They named their group the Harry Benjamin International Gender Dysphoria Association, Inc. I can't help but consider that putting "dysphoria" in the association title was a not-so-subtle shot across the bow directed at the American Psychiatric Association: "You mess with us; we will simply write our own standards."

The optics of the Standards of Care made it look like the gender activists wanted to effectively make the DSM-III irrelevant in diagnosing transgenders and directing treatment.

It is my thesis that Dr. Money's narcissistic, reckless disregard of psychological and psychiatric disorders in patients with gender issues and his bullheaded insistence to treat them with sex change on demand then and by others in the medical community now, has led to the high rate of transgenders committing and attempting suicide. Sex change on demand is not the right treatment for their disorders.

No standards of care have ever been drafted to protect the interests of the one undergoing gender surgery. The truth is the standards are to protect the doctors and surgeons, not the transgender. To illustrate this I'll share what the website of a prominent "Genital Reassignment Surgeon" says:

> "In general, despite misgivings about the Standards of Care, Dr. Bowers is required by the hospital and insurers to require two letters of approval...Our rigid adherence to a standard of care allows Dr. Bowers to retain insurance."

21

Two letters of approval. That's what this surgeon considers "rigid" adherence to the standards. And why does this surgeon require the letters? To retain insurance and have protection from culpability and legal liability. Not to determine the best treatment for the patient. In other words, to be able to pass the buck. If the patient ever regrets having surgery, the surgeon is off the hook.

Having a letter written does not mean that any of the guidelines in the standards were followed by the patient. The letters of approval are written by gender therapists, who can apply as much or as little of the standards as they care to. Approval can be granted without regard for the comorbid psychological and psychiatric disorders. In far too many cases, an approval letter merely justifies why a patient did not follow the standards.

I was approved by Dr. Walker twice, first in 1981 when I did not go through with surgery, and again in 1983 when I did have the surgery.[13] Openly homosexual, Walker prolifically drafted surgery approval letters. I was just one in a long list who got an approval letter from him. As a Dr. Walker client in 1981 and 1983 my personal experience is: He ignored all the guidelines in the standards he himself drafted. I can only conclude he and all the others who drafted the standards knew in 1979 that applying them, even fully and entirely, would not improve outcomes. Only recently I learned that Walker's degree was in social psychology, not clinical psychology. With that

---

[13] You can read Walt's story in its entirety: *Trading My Sorrows*, by Walt Heyer, Xulon Press, 2006, tradingmysorrows.com

degree, he was hardly qualified to evaluate underlying secondary disorders.

Walker never asked me about my childhood environment to see if it could have caused the onset of my gender disorder, like the DSM-III suggested. In the two fifty-minute sessions we had, he talked about his skiing accident and the transgender bars he frequented like the Roadrunner Bar in the San Francisco Tenderloin district. By not asking about my childhood, he missed hearing about the purple chiffon evening dress my grandma made for me, the heavy discipline by my mom and dad, and the fondling and touching I endured at the hands of my uncle. Without learning of my childhood abuse, he was incapable of diagnosing the comorbid dissociative disorder I had. If only Dr. Walker had followed the DSM-III in my case, needless surgery could have been avoided.

Now 30 years later, after writing books and getting a boat-load of emails from sex change regretters and their families, I have discovered that Dr. Walker was not the only one to ignore the childhood issues in his clients. It has been the unwritten rule of treatment to ignore any childhood issues and all psychiatric comorbid disorders and push the client solely toward gender transition.

The war over the word "disorder" that started back in 1979 lasted a long time and is now over—in the latest version of the DSM, Version 7, the word "disorder" is out; "dysphoria" is in.

The activists who pushed for this change should look up the word "dysphoria" because they will be dismayed to see it is defined as "an emotional state characterized by anxiety and depression." Anxiety and depression are both considered disorders, so who won the *war of the word* anyway?

More importantly today we have growing evidence transgenders suffer from psychological and psychiatric disorders as a direct result of childhood development. Brain and hormone theories continue to be disproved, leaving only psychological disorders.

Some will say the American Psychiatric Association caved in to political and social pressures when they removed "disorder" from the DSM. And no doubt they did cave to the political pressure. The word "disorder" will be gone but within the transgenders' fragile, untreated psyches the disorders will remain. There will be no noticeable reduction in suicides.

It's a Mental Disorder

4

*My son saw a psychologist and after one or two 50 minute visits
with her she diagnosed him as a transgender.*[14]

We know transgenders suffer from gender dysphoria. This
condition is characterized by troubling emotional issues like
anxiety, depression, and gender unease.[15] If, like me, you know
firsthand how quickly and easily this diagnosis is made, you
also know that often it is the only diagnosis that is even
considered, and only one treatment exists in everyone's
minds—radical, irreversible gender surgery.

My counselor in his evaluation of me for surgery had
focused solely on gender identity disorder. If he had taken the
time to dig further, he would have discovered my alcoholism

---

[14] "Transgender / ADHD" by Mary Alice, circa 2011, downloaded from
http://www.kristen-mcclure-therapist.com/transgender-adhd.html
on March 30, 2013

[15] http://www.thefreedictionary.com/Dysphoria

and heard the details of the abuse I suffered in my childhood. Either of these factors should have sounded a warning. He may not have had the expertise to diagnose the underlying dissociative disorder, but as one who wrote approval letters for surgery, he should have taken care to arrive at a proper diagnosis. The two overlooked issues became the foundation for my post-surgical regret and my considering suicide.

As we examine the high rate of suicide in the transgender population we need to consider how the rush to diagnose people with the first condition that pops into mind—gender dysphoria—plays into the tragic outcomes.

It's basic, really. The accuracy of the diagnosis is vitally important to the outcome because the diagnosis determines the path of treatment. The quick assumptions often made in diagnosing gender issues can lead to improper treatment and therapies, up to and including unnecessary surgery.

Improper treatment and needless surgery on perfectly good body parts can lead to regret and depression, and possibly suicide. And failure to address the original emotional issues means that the original emotional issues remain.

As of this writing, my own gender surgery was performed 30 years ago, with many post-surgery consequences remaining, some troubling; all caused by the surgery that cannot be undone. Some good eventually came out of it—27 years of sober living and 16 years of marriage as of this writing. For sure, I do not give up easily when it gets tough. But back to the truth that becomes an old ugly reality.

You can see in this randomly chosen letter on the internet from a mother how childhood issues are routinely ignored and therapists rush to diagnose gender clients:

My son was a normal 23 year old college student that was diagnosed with ADHD [Attention Deficit Hyperactivity Disorder]a little over two years ago. He has been medicated since then.

In the fall of last year out of the blue with NO behavior, indication, symptom, told us that he is a transgender. He had a normal childhood with regular ups and downs and never displayed an interest in dressing or acting out as a girl.

The family history has a few (2) suicides and bipolar in his father, his uncle, his paternal grandmother and a cousin on his mother's (me) side of the family.

He saw a psychologist and after one or two 50 minute visits with her she diagnosed him as a transgender. We went to meet with her to try and understand how she arrived at this diagnosis so quickly. She told us that she ran a list through her head and saw that he made more eye contact and was happier when she agreed that he was transgender.[16]

This mother's experience is not an exception; I often get these kinds of letters from transgenders and their family members and friends. It typifies how flippantly the diagnosis of gender dysphoria is made and how psychologists fail to explore the family history. It struck a chord with me because I, too, was diagnosed as a transgender after two 50-minute sessions. Thirty years ago it happened to me and two years ago to this 23 year old.

---

[16] "Transgender / ADHD" by Mary Alice, op. cit.

Using eye contact as a diagnostic measurement? This therapist did not explore any deeper issues, neither did mine 30 years ago. It is impossible for any therapist to accurately diagnose gender dysphoria or the underling causes such as ADHD or other factors in two sessions. This kind of "counseling" is reckless, foolish nonsense.

This 23 year old should be considered a ticking time bomb for suicide. A good therapist would ask all patients about any other illnesses they have and that exist in their family. A good therapist would agree that evaluating someone by eye contact is little more that witchcraft, not sound medical practice. Such a quickie diagnosis is quackery and can move a 23 year old into the suicide danger zone.

These activist therapists deliver the "you are a transgender" diagnosis all across this country but have no clue or desire to examine childhood issues. Deeper disorders remain unresolved and more accurate in-depth assessments are needed. The psychological issues that present as gender distress are multi-layered and often involve very complex disorders. The diagnosis process should never be a quick "slam bam" take some hormones and off to surgery you go.

I believe that those therapists who give a quick diagnosis of transgender rely heavily on income derived from the transgender community. They refuse to acknowledge any other well-founded evaluations or diagnoses because their income would suffer. Rather than the practice of medicine it begins to look like a cult or a con.

If someone you love goes to a medical professional for help with gender issues and comes out with a quick diagnosis, tell them to stop and get a new psychologist, someone who is not an activist for surgery, who will take the time to make an accurate assessment and diagnosis that become sound treatment. Many issues masquerade as gender dysphoria. Applying the radical treatment for gender dysphoria—hormones and surgery—to some other psychological malady can result in the amputation of perfectly good genitals. Find a medical professional who will take the time to learn what other issues are present and treat those first in an appropriate manner before jumping into an irreversible surgical procedure.

I get sad letters from parents, spouses of transgenders and transgenders themselves. In so many of them, the transgender has underlying issues that are not being addressed in the treatment modality. In letters I receive, the family members can clearly see the missed psychosis and the train wreck that is sure to follow transition. Sadly by the time the transgenders themselves can see it, it is usually later, sometimes years later, long after hormones and surgery.

The following story shows how a vulnerable man in the UK, depressed after losing his job, was led down the path to surgery.

> Gary Norton, 75, is pleading with the National Health Service to turn her from a woman back into a man, after realizing the sex change operation she had 23 years ago was a huge mistake. "I was vulnerable and I was given poor advice which has ruined my life. I don't want this to happen to anyone else."

Gary's horror story began when she sought help for depression from her GP after being laid off. During the meeting she admitted to dressing in her wife's clothes for a secret thrill. She says she now realizes this was as far as she ever wanted to go.

But she claims her GP concluded she could have been depressed because she wanted to be a woman and advised her to start taking hormone pills. Her GP referred her to a psychiatrist who diagnosed Gary as suffering from gender identity disorder and suggested she consider a sex change.

"I went along with it because I trusted them and thought they must be right even if I had never considered myself trapped in the wrong body before. Looking back I think all the female hormones had fuddled my mind. I want to advise others to think twice, it's one heck of a mistake to make and as I have found out there is no going back. In my mind I was misdiagnosed and should not have been operated on. "

In 1990 one year after the operation she wrote to her psychiatrist for help saying the operation had been a mistake and asked if she could have it reversed.

"He replied to say I needed to get on with it and embrace life as woman and make a success of it. What choice did I have?"

In the years that followed she took up modeling and dance classes, but no matter what she did Gary never felt like a woman.

"I passed well as a woman and those who knew said they all thought I had been born that way. But I always felt it was an act. I was pretending waiting for it to feel 'right' but it never did."

Eventually after 23 miserable years she had had enough of living a lie, stopped taking pills to let her facial hair grow back and started dressing as Gary again. [17]

It's astounding how easy it was for Gary to get surgery. He sought help for depression after getting laid off from his job, admitted to cross-dressing, and as a result was diagnosed by a psychiatrist with gender identity disorder. He was put on hormones which clouded his judgment and he underwent surgery. It is so sad: the regret, the pain, and the years he wasted as he tried to make it work. What a difference in people's lives could result if both therapist and client would take the time to make a complete diagnosis.

---

[17] Kelly Strange, "Gary Norton, 75, who became a woman in sex change operation 23 years ago wants to be a man again", Daily Mail, Published by Associated Newspapers Ltd, 27 November 2012, http://www.dailymail.co.uk/news/article-2239120/Gary-Norton-75-woman-sex-change-operation-23-years-ago-wants-man-again.html#ixzz2WzLYaBv1

No Protection for the Client

5

The standards of care have not been effective in preventing
regret or reducing deaths from suicide.
—Walt Heyer, the maverick transgender

At this point in the discussion, people with some familiarity with the transgender community will usually say, "But what about the Standards of Care? [18] What about the two year trial period of living as the desired gender before being approved for surgery?"

Based on my experience and the experiences of those who write to me, the Standards of Care make good window dressing, nothing more. One thing to know about the original Standards of Care, as well as their successor, is that they are merely suggestions to consider, not requirements. Nowhere in the U.S. will you find any enforcement of the approval process

---

[18] WPATH Standards of Care, op. cit.

for gender surgery: not for the transgenders or for the medical professionals who provide their care. No enforcement of the standards, not at all.

Most surgeons require a letter of approval from a psychologist. In my personal case, I happened to select the most well-known gender sexologist in the country at the time, Dr. Paul Walker. He was the guy who drafted and developed the original Harry Benjamin Standards of Care in 1979, the treatment guide for transgenders, which includes the criteria for approving individuals for gender change surgery.

In my case Dr. Walker's approval process was like the one hour motel; it was "slam, bam and thank you," not asking any questions that would have raised concerns about the possibility of comorbid disorders. As a result he did not discover my undiagnosed dissociative disorder or that I had been abused as a child emotionally, sexually and physically. If the dissociative disorder had been discovered it would most likely have made gender surgery unnecessary, or at the least, delayed it until much later. But Dr. Walker did no such diagnostic work and went forward, approving my gender changing surgery.

Walker wrote my approval letter to Dr. Stanley Biber that allowed Biber to perform the radical, irreversible gender surgery. The quick approval process demonstrated by Dr. Walker in my case has become the model and remains the most popular choice for many American therapists who end up quickly writing letters approving gender surgery for their clients.

As I said earlier, Dr. Walker diagnosed me in 1981 with gender identity disorder and approved me for surgery. I didn't go through with it that time. But he had another bite at the apple when I visited him again in 1983. Dr. Walker approved me for surgery not once, but on two separate occasions two years apart, saying I was suffering from gender identity disorder or as it is now called in its softer version, gender dysphoria.

Not only was I present at ground zero in Dr. Walker's office in the early days when he was developing the Standards of Care, I am still around to give voice to how long this foolishness has lasted and how the absolute foolishness needs to stop.

My case is not at all an isolated mistake; in fact, mistakes are common, even when the standards are followed completely. Here is a recent example of a letter I received showing that revision of the Standards of Care over time has done nothing to improve the outcomes from changing genders.

A physician, a man, became a transgender woman and told me he followed every step of the Standards of Care. This physician engaged the top surgeon in the U.S., the successor to my own Dr. Biber, Dr. Marci Bowers, who requires the standards be followed prior to surgery. Only six years post gender surgery the physician says to me in a letter:

If I could only go back to the day before my surgery in March of 2005—I would run from that surgeon's knife. I have lived and worked as a surgically altered man trying to play the part of a woman for 6 years. I spared no expense at trying to make it work.

This physician has since restored his male identity and regrets ever undergoing the gender change surgery.

The Standards of Care will not prevent the approval of an individual for surgery nor do they prevent regret or suicide, no matter how rigorously they are applied.

No punishments, loss of license, or consequences apply to those in the medical community who contribute to the failures.

I've heard a prominent surgeon whose thriving practice is based on transgender surgery say he doesn't know of any regret or suicide among his patients, even when I presented him with the evidence of regret in one of his own patients! It defies belief. What he means, of course, is that he doesn't want to know or admit it even when he knows because it is bad for his very lucrative business.

No tracking of outcomes is required. The Standards of Care do not even suggest that surgeons and psychologists track outcomes over time, so no one has any objective idea of how many are failures. That works to the advantage of those who want the surgery to continue. Everyone feels free to speculate about the numbers of success or failure and they do. I've heard reporters in the media declare "Regret is rare" with no evidence to back it up while ignoring the mountain of evidence that points to high rates of suicide.

The stories of regret come to me from all over the world and it is becoming very clear that the standards are a political activist tool but not worthy of any application in the treatment of gender identity disorders. Sadly, it is true. The guidelines do nothing to offend anyone or to discourage anyone from changing genders. I sure wish Dr. Walker would have discouraged me, or looked harder for the cause of my distress. That would have saved me and my children thirty years of heartache none of us needed.

I believe clinicians reach a diagnosis in widely varying ways, depending on whether or not they themselves are surgically transgendered and whether they support surgery. Precious few psychologists understand regret and suicide; few try hard to help the gender troubled by moving slowly and taking a cautious approach to treatment in an attempt to avoid poor outcomes.

The Standards of Care, if applied at all, are applied with too much liberal flexibility to be effective in recommending any treatment other than surgery. The standards themselves acknowledge:

> *The Standards of Care Are Flexible Clinical Guidelines*
>
> The SOC are intended to be flexible in order to meet the diverse health care needs of transsexual, transgender, and gender nonconforming people.[19]

The flexibility built into the Standards of Care is meant to protect the medical providers, not the patients. The Standards of Care give medical practitioners the flexibility to ignore, dismiss and not treat other serious disorders. Nowhere in the Standards of Care will you find any rigid guidelines for the prevention of suicide. In my view, that is reckless.

---

[19] WPATH Standards of Care, op. cit., p.2

The Standards of Care list a range of mental health concerns and urge screening for them:

> Clients presenting with gender dysphoria may struggle with a range of mental health concerns...
>
> Possible concerns include anxiety, depression, self-harm, a history of abuse and neglect, compulsivity, substance abuse, sexual concerns, personality disorders, eating disorders, psychotic disorders, and autistic spectrum disorders...
>
> Mental health professionals should screen for these and other mental health concerns and incorporate the identified concerns into the overall treatment plan.[20]

Notice that it doesn't say, "Don't do surgery on individuals actively suffering from any of these health concerns." It says to "incorporate the concerns into the overall treatment plan." The overall treatment plan always seems to include hormone treatment and surgery. The only cautionary note I can find is on page 62: "No surgery should be performed while a patient is actively psychotic."[21]

Well, that's a relief!

When I attended group sessions with a gender therapist who approved people for surgery, everyone in that group was obviously suffering from a mental disorder. The therapist did

---

[20] WPATH Standards of Care, op. cit., p. 24-25
[21] WPATH Standards of Care, op. cit., p. 62

not address any of those issues, but instead gave instruction on how to best present one's self as a woman with sessions on make-up, voice, dressing, walking, and so forth. Not exactly the in-depth analysis you'd expect.

I have struggled for over thirty years from the consequences of the gender change and it all started in Walker's office in 1981. I trusted him because he was the gender expert.

The WPATH Standards of Care are widely cited by medical professionals seeking to avoid any liability for sorrowful outcomes. I feel it is so important to share who, how, why and when the WPATH Standards of Care became the tool that guides hormone therapy and the approval for gender change surgery.

In 1966, the first public report of gender surgery in the U.S. started the gender madness in earnest. Johns Hopkins Hospital had opened a gender clinic in 1965 with Dr. John Money, sexologist and psychologist, on staff, to investigate and treat patients with gender identity disorder. Dr. Money made the proposition that gender was learned, not innate, and he spent his career trying to prove it. His theory was that if someone wanted to be a different gender he or she could learn to become that gender and all would be well.

Dr. Money happened upon the perfect case in 1967 to prove his theory, the Reimer twins. The penis of one of the boys was destroyed in a botched circumcision and his parents reached out to Dr. Money after seeing him interviewed on television. Dr. Money persuaded the parents to allow a gender change be performed on their *22-month-old* boy and to raise him as a girl. Money had the perfect set-up for proving nurture and social influences, not nature, determined gender.

Here is where we open the dark window into the onset of gender madness we know today as a sex change. We can even link suicide to changing genders as far back as the Reimer case.

Over the years Money wrote numerous journal articles, picked up by a willing media, where he touted the complete success of the experiment of boy turned girl. He built his reputation and career on that case. For thirty years, his view influenced the entire psychological community. Dr. Money was greatly admired for his gender work, why I do not know. Like the children lured by the Pied Piper of Hamelin to their deaths, gender change advocates mindlessly followed this man Money.

From all I can find Dr. Money was a deeply troubled, twisted and conflicted man regarding gender. He was an advocate of homosexuality and normalizing pedophilia as well as changing genders. Money lied about the results of his Reimer twins experiment. The truth eventually came out but it was after Bruce had suffered a severe toll on his emotional health. Bruce released a startling account of his upbringing and sessions with his psychologist Dr. Money. The boy Bruce, being raised as the girl Brenda, suffered from severe depression by the age of 9. The truth was that he had never adapted to being female and began living as a male in his teens. He was born a boy, always felt like a boy, and no amount of nurturing by his parents during his childhood convinced him otherwise. Unfortunately, Bruce committed suicide at age 38.

Like Reimer I also have gone public and released a book about my horrible story involving Dr. Walker. But few have listened. Can this book wake up the sleeping giants of psychiatry and psychology?

The gender advocates knew in 1979 suicide rates were high and success was low and still they went forward, undaunted, pushing for gender madness:

1) In 1979 a colleague of Harry Benjamin, Dr. Charles Ihlenfeld, reported 80% of the people did not need surgery and too many were committing suicide.[22]

2) Dr. Money was known for reporting success when no success was there to report. Even when faced with facts he refused to acknowledge he was wrong.[23]

3) Johns Hopkins Hospital's study of the results in transgenders from their clinic[24] proved so devastating the clinic was closed: no more sex changes were performed at Hopkins.

So, out of anger, stupidity or unabashed narcissism in 1979 the megalomaniac Dr. Money pushed for development of the

---

[22] Garrett Oppenheim, Ph.D., "Ihlenfeld Cautions On Hormones", *TRANSITION*, No. 8 - January/February 1979 Copyright 1979 - TRANSITION/ SOURCE: J2CP Information Services. Downloaded on 4/30/2013 from http://lvtgw.jadephoenix.org/Info_htm/Herbal_G/ginko_b2.htm

[23] Colapinto, John, *As Nature Made Him: The Boy Who Was Raised as a Girl*, Harper Perennial, 2011

[24] Meyer, J., and Reter, D. (1979). Sex reassignment. *Arch. Gen. Psychiat.* 36: 1010-1015.

Standards of Care to expand the gender surgery. In summary, the Standards of Care happened in this way:

> Who—Dr. Money persuaded his friend, Dr. Paul Walker, to write the 1979 Standards of Care after the Hopkins Clinic closed.

> How—Dr. Walker, a homosexual, gathered advocates, including an advocate of pedophilia, to write the Harry Benjamin Standards of Care.

> Why—I think Dr. Money, Benjamin and Dr. Walker in the face of all the evidence pointing to gender change failure ignored it because they wanted to make their mark on history.

> When—in 1979 in San Diego, California, the first draft of the Standards of Care were drafted. In 2013, the 7th version was released.

With a staggering suicide death rate for transgenders I think we can conclude that neither the DSM nor the Standards of Care have been effective. The DSM now joins the Standards of Care as another piece of activist propaganda to advance the transgender social change agenda.

Next we will explore the real reasons for suicide.

90% of Suicides

6

If you are suicidal, you probably are suffering
from clinical depression, bipolar disorder,
schizophrenia, postpartum depression, PTSD,
or something similar.[25]
–Kevin Caruso, Executive Director of Suicide.org

Research has shown that more than 90 percent of people who kill themselves have depression or another diagnosable mental or substance abuse disorder, often in combination with other mental disorders.[26]

---

[25] Suicide.org, *Suicide Causes*, by Kevin Caruso, referenced on May 5, 2013

[26] New York State Office of Mental Health, "SPEAK about: Suicide questions and answers", first printed May 2004, revised March 2007, references the following two studies for this statement: Moscicki EK. Epidemiology of completed and attempted suicide: toward a framework for prevention. Clinical Neuroscience Research, 2001; 1: 310-23; Conwell Y, Brent D. Suicide and aging. I: patterns of

Why should the cause of suicide among transgenders be any different? It doesn't take a rocket scientist to reason that the psychiatric disorders present in those who kill themselves in the population as a whole must be considered as a cause for suicide among transgenders. Yet, as hard as it is to believe, the psychiatric disorders that are strongly associated with being suicidal are commonly left undiagnosed and untreated in the transgender population. Often, they are not even talked about.

Why not? The reasons are very simple:

1. The LGBT agenda rules the social and political climate. They don't want the word disorder, much less the phrase mental disorder, associated with their agenda.
2. Individual transgenders reject the idea that they could have a mental disorder.
3. The medical community that caters to transgenders rushes to treat them with hormones and surgery.
4. Suicide is hushed up, unless it can be blamed on bullying or discrimination to help the activist agenda, even though they are not the predominant causes of suicide.

My conclusion: Without a doubt, the high rate of suicide among transgenders is due to the lack of diagnosis and treatment of the coexisting disorders that cause suicide such as *depression or other diagnosable mental or substance abuse disorders.*

The statistics for suicide are the same before and after gender transition. The reason could be that transition doesn't

---

psychiatric diagnosis. International Psychogeriatrics,1995; 7(2): 149-64.

make any other disorder disappear. Underlying issues are still there after transition and still require treatment. Suicides will continue at an alarming rate until the first line of care is to discover the messy comorbid (coexisting) disorders and rigorously apply treatment to them.

Transgenders have many psychological triggers that drive the desire to change from one gender to another. I can tell you now that my own desire for gender transition was to escape being a boy. I did not like being the young boy who was frequently crossed-dressed by my grandma in girl's dresses and disciplined by my dad with spankings on my young tender butt with a hardwood floor plank. It was not fun being the little boy Uncle Fred enjoyed teasing and *touching me down there.* It was not fun being the small kid who was called names. For me it was vital to escape into a gender no one would hurt, tease or call names. I did not see people hurting girls like they hurt me. So I became a female at first in my head.

Escaping my birth gender was a way to cope with my deeper troubles which went undiagnosed. My gender disorder no doubt was real but under it was another layer. I learned many years after my surgery that I suffered from a dissociative disorder, which is not uncommon in the transgender spectrum of disorders. Surgery does not resolve a dissociative disorder; in fact I have been told surgery is not only unnecessary, it makes it harder to recover.

There is no doubt comorbid disorders will leave the mental health professional in a quandary as to which diagnosis should be treated first and many opt for treating the gender dysphoria first with hormones or surgery. In my view, comorbid disorders should be diagnosed and treated first, before administering hormone therapy or surgery, for the following reasons.

First, we know messing with a person's hormone levels can predispose them to depression and suicide.[27] Preventing suicide should have priority over all other medical considerations.

Second, some of the other disorders have symptoms that look like gender issues. Treat the comorbid issue and the gender issues can be treated with something other than surgery.

How prevalent is the coexistence of other disorders with gender dysphoria? According to a survey of Dutch psychiatrists published in the *American Journal of Psychiatry* cross-gender identification was comorbid with other psychiatric disorders for 61% of the patients (359 people). The comorbid disorders they reported in their clients were personality disorders, major mood disorders, psychotic disorders and dissociative disorders, like was true in my own case.[28]

Another research study looked at psychiatric comorbidity in gender identity disorder (GID) and found that forty-two percent (42%) of the patients were diagnosed with one

---

[27] Asscheman H, Gooren LJ, Eklund PL., "Mortality and morbidity in transsexual patients with cross-gender hormone treatment", op. cit.

[28] Joost à Campo, M.D.; Henk Nijman, Ph.D.; H. Merckelbach, Ph.D.; Catharine Evers, M.Sc., "Psychiatric Comorbidity of Gender Identity Disorders: A Survey Among Dutch Psychiatrists", *The American Journal of Psychiatry* July, 2003; 160:1332-1336. 10.1176/appi.ajp.160.7.1332 Downloaded from http://ajp.psychiatryonline.org/article.aspx?articleID=176330

or more personality disorders. Their conclusion is that lifetime psychiatric comorbidity in GID patients is high, and this fact should be taken into account in the assessment and treatment planning.[29]

As we explore some of the many psychological and psychiatric issues associated with transgenders, not all of the disorders are layered into every transgender. No doubt you will discover one or more of the disorders will be a good fit with a transgender you know. Perhaps it won't be any of the ones presented here, but it is definitely worth exploring the idea of comorbidity when someone you love is in the midst of a life-threatening trial.

Let's take a look at more illnesses, some with known links to suicide ideation, which could be hiding within the gender dyphoric patient, starting with the big one, depression.

DEPRESSION

Untreated depression is the number one cause for suicide. Depression is often directly associated with negative experiences or triggers. I endured 15 out of the 21 common triggers for depression—and that almost drove me to suicide. So I can tell you from my own experience the triggers shown in the list below are common among individuals who elect to transition from one gender to another.

---

[29] J. Hepp, B. Kraemer, U. Schnyder, N. Miller, A. Delsignore, "Psychiatric comorbidity in gender identity disorder", *Journal of Psychosomatic Research*, Volume 58, Issue 3 , pages 259-261, March 2005. Downloaded from http://www.jpsychores.com/article/S0022-3999(04)00595-1/abstract

Depression Triggers

1. Divorce, separation, or break up of a relationship (this could include family and friends) *
2. Losing custody of children or feeling the decision about custody is not fair *
3. A serious loss, such as job, house or ability to earn income *
4. Intense emotional pain *
5. Loss of hope *
6. Physical abuse
7. Verbal abuse
8. Unresolved abuse from the past as a child *
9. Feeling trapped in a perceived negative situation *
10. Feeling things will never get better *
11. Feeling hopeless *
12. Serious legal problems
13. Feeling you have been taken advantage of *
14. Inability to effectively cope with a perceived humiliating situation
15. Inability to deal with perceived failure *
16. Alcohol abuse *
17. Drug abuse *
18. The feeling you are not accepted by family and friends *
19. A horrible disappointment *
20. Being bullied
21. Having low self-esteem

Source: Caruso, Kevin, "Suicide Causes", suicide.org

* indicates experiences from the author's life

Extreme stress can overwhelm the best of us and I became suicidal after my gender change surgery. Deeply depressed at times and ecstatic at other times, I started to plan how I could take my life, thinking suicide would be the only way to avoid lifelong failure and regret.

I have learned over the years that depression is common among transgenders. Being depressed puts the person at greater risk of suicide, and gender surgery may only temporarily provide relief. Often the person will have a reduced desire for medical care, including medications. If not properly treated, the depression can, and most often will, worsen. Therefore it is essential to recognize and diagnose depression early and apply adequate, appropriate treatment to prevent as many suicides as possible.

RESISTANCE TO TREATMENT: COULD IT BE NARCISSISM?

Transgenders tend to want relief from their distress and they want it now. They go to extreme lengths to get hormones, often from back alley type of practitioners who ask no questions. They seek out quick approval for surgery, or they travel to other countries where no approval is necessary. They ignore the reactions of family and friends, preferring to pursue surgery over relationships. They scream for acceptance and reject any rational advice to slow down and rule out other disorders before undergoing surgery.

I often wonder why. What would cause a person to so strongly resist all traditional means of medical care and seek out such a bizarre life change? I'm not a psychologist or psychiatrist, so some may think my ideas are naïve but who knows? Maybe in this case, as they say, "out of the mouths of babes" come wisdom and truth. You can follow my line of reasoning and see if it resonates with anyone you know.

I heard from a transgender man whose therapist, amazingly, is thoroughly exploring his underlying issues first, and looking for what is driving the man's desire to change from male to female. The client willingly participated in the hard work of therapy and is very pleased he avoided unnecessary genital surgery. This is how counseling should work to prevent surgery and possibly suicide. The man shares what his therapist thinks motivated him so strongly to change genders:

I still hear that psychoanalyst's voice telling me that my desire to change genders and become a woman was a defense against anxieties about being with a woman socially, romantically or sexually. For years she told me that I was trying to change my gender so I could become the object of my own affection and desire.

When I read the phrase "the object of my own desire" I went looking for any possible link between transgender suicide and narcissism. The more I read and consider a connection between narcissism and transgenders, the more it becomes evident that the definition of narcissist describes the behavior of many transgenders.

Narcissism is an inflated self-image and addiction to fantasy[30] and exhibits the elements of self-love, self-involvement

---

[30] The Encyclopedia Britannica,
   http://www.britannica.com/EBchecked/topic/403456/narcissism

and self destruction.[31] Narcissist people have an abnormally elevated level of self-admiration.

Oxford Dictionaries defines a narcissist as someone who has an "excessive or erotic interest in oneself and one's physical appearance." Narcissists demonstrate "extreme selfishness, with a grandiose view of one's own talents and a craving for admiration." [32]

√ If you are around transgenders even for a short time, you will see that the obsession about their physical appearance is at the very core of their lives.

In the DSM-IV, we see that narcissists share traits that are also identified with transgender individuals. Narcissists believe they are "special"—different and unique—and cannot be understood by "regular" people. They have a sense of entitlement, unreasonable expectations, and always expect special treatment.[33] Narcissists try to devalue others' achievements and have a delusional belief that others are envious of them.

√ Transgenders, who do not comply with social gender norms, have similar thinking.

An entry about narcissism in the revised DSM-V under the heading "pathological personality trait" caught my eye:

---

31 Edward Shorter, *A Historical Dictionary of Psychiatry,* Oxford University Press, Feb 17, 2005; p. 184

32 Oxford Dictionaries, Oxford University Press, 2013, http:// oxforddictionaries.com/us/definition/american_english/narcissism

33 Diagnostic and Statistical Manual of Mental Disorders Fourth edition Text Revision (DSM-IV-TR) American Psychiatric Association (2000)

"Attention seeking: excessive attempts to attract and be the focus of the attention of others; admiration seeking." [34]

√ Transgenders and some cross-dressers require excessive admiration and reassurance of their appearance. We see the overt exaggeration of excessive make up, over the top dress outfits in the style of homosexual drag queens.

Narcissism has been identified as the fear of being "normal" or being like everybody else. Narcissists will get frustrated and/or argue to the death to prove that he/she is special and different if challenged. Almost as to prove themselves to be different the narcissist will strive toward antisocial tendencies and disagrees with and/or disregards many of the social norms.

√ Transgenders are the same. If you deny them the surgery, they will find someone else somewhere in the world that will do it.

Some researchers have suggested that narcissistic features can be found in those who have gender identity disorder.[35] A study published in the *International Journal of Trangenderism* says narcissistic pathology has been identified in the transgender

---

[34] To be published in May, 2013. The entry for narcissism was updated in June, 2011. *DSM-IV and DSM-5 Criteria for the Personality Disorders,* American Psychiatric Association (2012)

[35] Wilchesky, Marilyn; Cote, Helene; "Gender identity disorder: creative? Adaptive? Or absurd?" The Canadian Journal of Human Sexuality, 1996, Volume 5, Issue 4. Downloaded June 15, 2013, from http://www.biomedsearch.com/article/Gender-identity-disorder-creative-Adaptive/30412100.html

psyche: *We could identify a significant narcissistic pathology in most of our [gender dysphoric] patients...*[36]

Sam Vaknin, the author of the book, *Malignant Self Love: Narcissism Revisited,* speaks in particular about transsexual narcissists:

> Transsexual narcissists feel entitled to special treatment and cosseting, demonstrated in a grandiose sense of entitlement ("I deserve to be taken care of") and omnipotence ("I can be whatever I want to be – despite nature/God"). This feeling of entitlement is especially manifest in some gender dysphoric individuals who aggressively pursue hormonal or surgical treatment. They feel that it is their inalienable right to receive it on demand and without any strictures or restrictions. For instance, they oftentimes refuse to undergo psychological evaluation or treatment as a condition for receiving the hormonal or surgical treatment.[37]

---

[36] Hartmann U, Becker H, Rueffer-Hesse C (1997) Self and Gender: Narcissistic Pathology and Personality Factors in Gender Dysphoric Patients. Preliminary Results of a Prospective Study. IJT 1,1, http://www.symposion.com/ijt/ijtc0103.htm. Downloaded on 6/11/2013 from http://www.wpath.org/journal/www.iiav.nl/ezines/web/IJT/97-03/numbers/symposion/ijtc0103.htm

[37] Sam Vaknin, http://samvak.tripod.com/faq18.html

Perhaps you wonder why I have taken time to connect narcissism and transgenders. Out of all the narcissistic behaviors, three are most prevalent among transgenders:

First, rules do not apply in the world of narcissistic personality. This is why they challenge their gender and social gender norms.

Second, narcissistic personalities HATE being criticized even if you show some concern; that looks like criticism to a narcissist. Everything looks like criticism and bullying to them.

Third, they are resistant to facts. Nothing is ever their fault, even when faced with extraordinary evidence and proof. It will never, ever be their fault.

The similarities in behavior between transgenders and narcissists are striking. The case can be made that transsexualism evolves from deep narcissistic devotion to becoming a real woman and regret comes after surgery with the realization that a gender change is impossible. The timing of the regret is particularly devastating because parts were removed and cannot be retrieved and replaced as if nothing happened.

LET'S OUTLAW TALK THERAPY

Transgenders, as a rule, want to avoid talk therapy and they found a friend in California. Governor Jerry Brown signed into law a bill which prohibits therapists when working with a patient under 18 years of age to engaging in sexual orientation change efforts. It defines these efforts as any practices that seek to change an individual's sexual orientation, behaviors or gender expressions.[38]

This could be the proverbial camel nose under the tent. The next step could be to outlaw therapies to help transgender adults recover from their gender confusion and behaviors. Currently four other states are considering similar legislation.

This bill will make therapists think twice about assisting minors who are concerned about same sex attraction or are confused in their gender identity. If the child perceives the talk therapy as an attempt in any way to "cure them" of same sex attractions (homosexuality) or gender expression, the therapist will face loss of their license to practice.

Sadly, this new California "protection" bill will do far more to protect pedophiles from prosecution and leave minors unprotected from adults who prey on them. Predatory adult men who engage in homosexual acts with kids are sick. The activists pushed for the new law because they want it written into law that sodomy is good, even healthy, even with or by minors. That in my view is a mental disorder—sick, perverted and narcissistic; no mistake about that.

As a young child I unfortunately was molested by my uncle many times before the age of ten. I detested what my uncle did and it hurt me deeply and took a lot to learn to live

---

[38] California Legislative Information, Senate Bill No. 1172, version 9/30/2012, Chaptered by Secretary of State. Chapter 835, Statutes of 2012. Downloaded on June 15, 2013, from http://leginfo.legislature.ca.gov/faces/billNavClient.xhtml?bill_id=201120120SB1172

with. I may never completely overcome it because the event cannot be purged from my memory.

I feel this bill could effectively eliminate any and all talk therapy because, let's face it, any course of therapy could be accused of being one that seeks to change behavior. The science of psychotherapy continually progresses based on research and researchers and studies often contradict each other, only building to a consensus over many years through the free flow of ideas. That's what's so chilling about this bill. It legislates what a therapist may discuss with a client and which behaviors are considered changeable and which are not. It sets it in stone.

The results in one study of suicide attempts by lesbian, gay, bisexual, and transgender youth suggest the importance of addressing the depression and hopelessness that leads to suicide.[39] How does a therapist address depression and hopelessness if he or she is prohibited from exploring behaviors that are troubling the teenager?

I know on a personal level the need for talk therapy. My long journey with gender issues started at the age of 5 and continued into my teen years. It kept me wondering if I was homosexual because of what my uncle did to me. In some ways I did not want to grow up and become a man because I thought men did to kids what my uncle did to me and I hated that.

---

[39] Mustanski, Brian; Liu, Richard T., "A Longitudinal Study of Predictors of Suicide Attempts Among Lesbian, Gay, Bisexual, and Transgender Youth," Archives of Sexual Behavior, April 2013, Volume 42, Issue 3, pp 437-448. Downloaded on June 15, 2013 from http://link.springer.com/article/10.1007%2Fs10508-012-0013-9

Isn't it interesting the LGBT wants to eliminate the one thing that might have the ability to prevent suicide—talk therapy?

SUMMARY

I am shaken every time I hear of a transgender suicide because it could have been me. The medical community blindly ignores secondary psychological disorders. Admittedly, the process of identifying and treating coexisting issues is complicated and multi-layered. But to break the cycle of suicide and suicide attempts in this population, the hypothesis that narcissism, anxiety and depression are contributory psychological issues must be considered. Even this simple review of a few of the mostly untreated psychological issues helps us begin to understand why so many transgenders turn to suicide.

A law like California's that impairs or prevents talking to a therapist about homosexuality does not foster an atmosphere for recognizing coexisting depressive disorders. Certain and specific interviewing skills are required to recognize the need for both pharmacologic and psychotherapeutic treatments. When the guidelines are followed, patient outcomes are often quite good.

As I said early on in this chapter, transgender suicides will continue at an alarming rate until the first line of care is to discover the messy comorbid (coexisting) disorders and rigorously apply treatment to them. The WPATH Standards of Care need to include strong language elevating the diagnosis process to include psychiatric evaluations by a medical doctor that focuses on prevention of suicides, uncovering depressive disorders and preventing unnecessary surgeries.

I will continue to be the loud persistent voice of the suicide victims who have no voice.

Look, if the suicide attempts were not at 41% and I did not see over 43,000 hits on my web site, sexchangeregret.com, in 12 months and climbing, I would say nothing. But the suicides occur to real people who need real psychological help for their real disorders. They do not need to have their genitals handed over to a surgeon whose only regret is not performing more surgeries.

Are you getting aggravated yet about what is going on? We looked at the craziness of one state passing legislation to prevent talk therapy for minors with gender issues. In the next chapter we will look at the absurd idea that the high rate of suicide among transgenders is your fault.

It's Your Fault

7

The mission of the advocates is
to frame their social agenda as a civil rights issue.
—*Walt Heyer, the maverick transgender*

After living in the transgender community for eight years I reached this conclusion about gender change: It was never about providing treatment for gender issues like I had.

Gender, male or female—at the very core of who we are—is now being driven by an expanded LGBT agenda. They started long ago to blur the lines, pushing to normalize transgender gender sex and to eradicate distinctions between male and female genders. We see the success of their actions today in the acceptance of gender fluidity—or as they describe it: every day you may choose which gender you are for that day.

In their view, society, schools and businesses should play along with the person's delusion. To accomplish their political goals they need to force acceptance of the phony genders on everyone, like it or not. Convincing the majority is a big task, but they have proven themselves up for the challenge.

The handful of homosexuals who were pushing for gender change in the 60s, 70s, and 80s has morphed into a huge national army of well-financed political groups. The National Gay and Lesbian Task Force or as they call themselves "the Task Force," leads the charge. Its mission is:

> ...to build the grassroots power of the lesbian, gay, bisexual and transgender (LGBT) community. We do this by training activists, equipping state and local organizations with the skills needed to organize broad-based campaigns to defeat anti-LGBT referenda and advance pro-LGBT legislation, and building the organizational capacity of our movement.[40]

Transgender suicides are simply collateral damage, useful propaganda in the war to push for "civil rights" laws. Starting with the first draft of the Standards of Care authored by homosexual Dr. Paul Walker, the aim was *not* to help alleviate gender distress but to advance an agenda of acceptance for homosexuality, sodomy, non-conforming genders and repugnant sexual acts. (Please note: None of that was ever my desire or represented any behaviors I engaged in. I have always

---

[40] Grant, Jaime M., et. al., *Injustice at Every Turn: A Report of the National Transgender Discrimination Survey.* op. cit., page d

had the opinion that sodomy is very perverted. I am not homosexual; neither are many other transgenders.)

By lumping in the plight of the discriminated-against transgender with homosexuals, the LGBT can successfully fight for legislation to normalize the way society views and treats the abusive, violent and predatory practices of pornography, pedophilia and sodomy.

The mission of the advocates is to frame their social agenda as a civil rights issue. They are setting the stage for transgenders to appear no different than the African American slaves who picked cotton in the fields. The goal of their social indoctrination is to depict themselves as abused, shackled and enslaved by society, faith and all the old traditional gender norms. They claim they are being widely discriminated against and their civil rights are being violated in order to promote their progressive agenda.

The only thing missing from their argument was proof. In 2008, the National Gay and Lesbian Task Force joined with the National Center for Transgender Equality to conduct a survey of transgenders in the U.S. The purpose stated in the survey was:

> ...to bring the full extent of discrimination against transgender and gender non-conforming people to light.[41]

That's it. One goal: to show that transgenders are discriminated against.

---

[41] Ibid., page 2

In reading a study with such obvious bias and agenda, we have to put on our thinking caps and try to read it with an objective and scientific eye. Here are a few of the things that popped out at me, and I'm not a professional researcher by any means.

First thing to ask: how did they get the sample of people to survey? Is it representative? Is it random or does the selection process have a bias that might skew the results?

In this survey, the authors tell us straight out: "It is not appropriate to generalize the findings in this study to all transgender and gender non-conforming people *because it not a random sample.* [emphasis mine]" [42]

Why is a random sample important? As people in academia know, when a sample is not random, it will favor certain groups, possibly without the sampler even realizing it. When the sample is not representative of the population, any statistics and conclusions based on the sample are inappropriate for the larger population, no matter how large the number surveyed.

You can be sure that everyone is going to forget about that little admission *"it is not a random sample"* buried on page 13. Advocates everywhere will ignore the caution, generalize the findings to all transgender and gender non-conforming people, and refer to the findings as objective proof. It's too tempting.

Next, we want to know how this sample represents the U.S. population as a whole. Does it cover the same geographical

---

[42] Ibid., page 13

area? Does it match the age distribution? The survey tells us that they did a good job of geographic distribution, but not with age: "Our sample has a larger percentage of young people than the U.S. population as a whole [52% v. 36%]."[43] Twenty (20) percent are students.[44]

This becomes important as the authors draw their conclusions. They compare outcomes from their youth-weighted sample to the U.S. population as a whole, which is not a fair comparison. Think about students, for example. They are more likely to have a low income or be unemployed than non-students. The authors are using, as the expression goes, an "apples to oranges" comparison. Over time, advocates will use this information out of context to make their case and the media will report it as absolute fact rather than digging below the surface. It's too inconvenient and time-consuming to go and verify the statement against the source.

The report, which has the provocative title, *Injustice at Every Turn*, paints a bleak picture of the lives of the 6,450 transgenders included in the survey saying that "bias-related events lead to insurmountable challenges and devastating outcomes."

The use of the word "insurmountable" insults me as a person. I myself faced many of the challenges presented in the report, but to say the challenges are insurmountable is to say I am a victim with no power to influence my life. That is not the way I choose to live. I think this type of victimized thinking is

---

[43] Ibid., page 21
[44] Ibid., page 17

toxic. It gets internalized in those who have gender issues and leads to hopelessness and depression.

The questions in the survey are constructed so that every trial in the life of a transgender is related to suffering from bias. In their report they emphasize the results that support their agenda and preconceived goals and blame all of us for the "devastating outcomes" such as:

1. Respondents reported HIV infections four times the national average.

2. 70% reported drinking or misuse of drugs using as a coping mechanism.*

3. Almost 2% of respondents were currently homeless, which is almost twice the rate of the general population (1%).*

4. Survey respondents experienced unemployment at twice the rate of the general population at the time of the survey.*

5. Respondents lived in extreme poverty. Our sample was nearly four times more likely to have a household income of less than $10,000/year compared to the general population.*

6. 41% of respondents reported attempting suicide compared to 1.6% of the general population.*

I put a star (*) next to the challenges that I faced during and after my transition: all of them except HIV infection. I lived through the bias and discrimination imposed on me. It wasn't easy, but I surmounted these challenges, but then, I didn't blame discrimination and bias for my difficulties. I blamed myself for falling for the lie perpetrated by Dr. Walker, Dr.

Money, Dr. Biber, and all the others who followed in their footsteps who told me it was possible to surgically make myself a woman. I found out way too late I had been taken in by a fraud. We transgenders, in our confusion and extreme anxiety, allow ourselves to be deceived by the LGBT radical homosexual agenda, learning only after gender surgery it is impossible to surgically manufacture gender. Blaming others for the consequences of our decision only worsens our troubles.

Let's look closer at the listed outcomes and the discrimination the survey authors want us to believe is to blame.

HIV INFECTION

Blaming HIV infection on discrimination is a huge leap, I think. In the majority of cases, HIV infection is linked to unprotected anal intercourse or sharing needles with someone who is infected. Avoid these two high-risk behaviors and the likelihood of getting infected plummets. (I wasn't homosexual or an IV drug user and I didn't participate in those behaviors most likely to lead to HIV infection.)

DRINKING OR MISUSE OF DRUGS

Blaming drinking or misuse of drugs on anything, including "using as a coping mechanism," goes contrary to all 12-step recovery programs. In order to stop using, the addict has to stop blaming others.

HOMELESSNESS

Blaming homelessness on discrimination ignores the impact of drinking or misusing drugs on one's ability to hold onto a job and pay the rent.

UNEMPLOYMENT AND EXTREME POVERTY

Blaming unemployment on discrimination might hold some truth, but again, considering that the sample was heavily weighted with students and young people who are more likely to be unemployed, we don't have a proper sample on which to conclude anything. Plus the study acknowledged that 2008 was the beginning of high unemployment in general due to the economic recession and people were losing their jobs, transgender or not.

These topics are interesting, but not nearly as important to me as suicide. Let's explore some of the areas the task force missed and jumped out at me as extremely important.

SEXUAL ABUSE

The survey gives some startling information about the connection between sexual abuse and suicide attempts:

- √ Ten percent (10%) of respondents were sexually assaulted...[45]
- √ Sexual assault survivors reported a suicide attempt rate of 64%.[46]
- √ The suicide attempt rate was 69% among those who were sexually assaulted by teachers.[47]

---

[45] Ibid., page 80
[46] Ibid., page 83

What is glaringly absent from *Injustice at Every Turn* is an outcry to stop and prevent the sexual abuse which is driving suicide attempts. Maybe those who engage in homosexual behaviors and twisted sex activities are hesitant to call out the behavior of sexual predators?

MENTAL DISORDER

The bias of the authors and their agenda is seen clearly in how they approach the topic of mental health. Out of a survey of seventy (70) questions, only three (3) are related to mental health and those are quite general.

When I look at the survey for other signs of mental disorders, the answers to Question 3 jump out. Question 3 asked respondents to designate their primary gender identity today. Now you and I know there are two genders, male and female, but thirteen percent (13%) chose "a gender not listed here" as their answer, as shown in the results table:[48]

Q3. Primary Gender Identity Today

Male/Man	1687	26%
Female/Woman	2608	41%
Part time as one gender, part time as another	1275	20%
A gender not listed here, please specify	**864**	**13%**
Total	6434	100%

I'm shocked. The authors expected to get that answer; why else would they list it among the possible answers? Am I the only one who thinks a person might have mental health issues if they

---

[47] Ibid., page 45

[48] Ibid., page 16

describe their gender not as male or female but as "a gender not listed here"?

SUICIDE

The finding that 41% of respondents reported attempting suicide[49] is shown as one of three key findings in the Executive Summary and given a lot of attention, as it should. Compared to the 1.6% for the U.S. population, the rate is shocking. My conclusion differs from theirs, however. I believe the high rate should provide sufficient proof that a sex change is not effective as a treatment procedure. To me, it demonstrates that transgenders remain suffering from untreated psychological and psychiatric disorders. Yet the Report of the National Transgender Discrimination Survey did not consider psychological disorders as a possible cause.

The survey also points out that those respondents who *have* transitioned have higher rates of attempted suicide than those who *have not*. I could hardly believe what I was reading. That is a provocative finding, one that does not help the LGBT agenda. In reporting this finding, the authors provide no conclusions, no analysis, no commentary, nothing. The exact quote in its entirety is: "Those who have medically transitioned and surgically transitioned have higher rates of attempted suicide than those who have not."[50]

Maybe you read this like I do. When I see that those who transitioned had higher rates of attempted suicide, my head jerks up. I immediately wonder why. In my mind, this finding

---

[49] Ibid., page 2
[50] Ibid., page 82

raises the possibility that transitioning is detrimental for some. Perhaps transitioning is not effective as a treatment procedure.

But from the authors of the report, only silence. The gender change political groups are walking right past the gravestones of transgenders who committed suicide because for them, political power is far more exciting than dead transgenders. Suicides offer an opportunity to portray transgenders as victims of social injustice and discrimination, which in turn is used as justification for new laws.

This extremely well-funded activist group prefers to use this psychologically troubled population as a pawn in their mission for new sexual civil rights. They will always see progressive social change as their primary focus all the while turning a blind eye to the alarmingly high transgender suicide rate. If the deaths and attempts were to become widely known and the advocates were forced to acknowledge that a gender change results in regret and suicide, their agenda would suffer.

Casting their constituency group as victims of society is a great fundraiser for the LGBT. Pulling the victim card is effective in persuading lawmakers to forge ahead with new civil rights laws for transgenders. But placing the responsibility and burden for transgenders' well-being, health, and quality of life on society will keep transgenders from assuming any responsibility. Blaming others, as I learned, has no benefit and only promotes a stereotype of "a damsel in distress," driving even lower their self esteem.

No doubt transgenders suffer from all kinds of stuff. I know I did for 8 years when I lived as Laura Jensen, but I did not blame anyone but myself. The new social protection laws, whether good or bad, will not help in improving their quality of life or in lowering their suicide rate.

The LGBT always spins the idea more laws are needed to protect them. The transgender advocates are mostly homosexual activists who have very little concern for heterosexual men who have gender identity issues. The inconvenient truth of the staggering suicide rates and psychiatric depression must, for the purposes of the activist agenda, remain hidden, suppressed, ignored and denied, even in medical research. Meanwhile, transgenders will continue to die from suicide because the surgical treatment will not alleviate the anxiety, depression or disorders.

We cower from the powerful sexual activist group and allow them to prevail in getting laws enacted that shove acceptance, tolerance and diversity down our throats. We are told we must hire them, give them special bathrooms, pay their medical costs and grant them legal privileges.

We don't even notice the absence of advocacy for medical care or research aimed at preventing their suicides. Transgender suicides are mainly the result of clinical psychological disorders, not, as the advocates say, the result of social homophobic discrimination leveled at transgenders.

The widespread systemic denial makes it tough for the scientific community to conduct research with freedom to follow the science where it leads. Serious repercussions are directed toward anyone who studies transgender health and has the courage to publish research results that run contrary to the agenda. Researchers in the medical community face professional ostracism and loud, virulent attacks from advocates who are intolerant of anything that runs counter to their view.

As a self-proclaimed maverick transgender, I don't have a professional career to protect, so I am free to say it as I see it. I look at the transgender suicides, depression and regret and realize the community has not been promoting a therapeutic ideology in the treatment of gender depression.

The advocates are so antagonistic toward being labeled as psychologically ill they lobbied to get the word "disorder" taken out of the diagnostic manual. Transgenders themselves don't want to be told they have a disorder. In fact, they do not want anyone diagnosing them; they prefer to diagnose themselves with gender dysphoria. Denial is the order of the day.

On the one hand, transgender advocates broadcast to the world that a sex change is wonderful, successful and leads to a much better life. But they turn their rhetoric on a dime to advance their civil rights agenda, claiming they are victims of anti-transgender bias, crime and racism. They claim a sex change is successful then tell us transgenders live in extreme poverty and 41% will attempt suicide and a disproportionate number will die from suicide. The slick-tongued devils talk out of both sides of their mouth when it helps their agenda.

They say transgenders just need more acceptance and tolerance from the rest of us. But when it looks like madness, and suicides prevail, that is very hard to accept or tolerate; at least too hard for me.

To me it looks like the activists will continue to flash their drag queen high heels seductively in front of lawmakers coast to coast, citing the survey as if it were scientific proof and use their new-found success in changing the DSM to move toward ever more expansive social civil rights protection laws.

In the next chapter, we'll see some personal stories that show why it's so important to get the diagnosis and treatment right.

Six-fold Regret

8

Many people who regret their surgery email me.
Thankfully, these are the lucky ones. At least they did
not take their life by suicide.
—*Walt Heyer, the maverick transgender*

Stories of regret are the proof that the standard practice of allowing the client to self-diagnose their gender dysphoria and recommend surgery as treatment has flaws. Perhaps by reading some of the emails, which I share with their permission, you will begin to see the bigger picture.

1 In this first story we see how quickly the regret arrived. He is male to female and writing to me four months post-op. Read about his experience in his own words:

I recently had the sex change surgery, and although I thought I was completely sure of what I was doing, I began to regret the decision a mere three weeks after the operation.

Some might say I was experiencing post-op depression, but it was definitely more than that. I also suspect that many of the other patients at the hospital who had the same operation experienced similar feelings based on my discussions with them.

What really drove the point home for me was the realization that it required eight hours on an operating table to make my genitalia appear to be female.

That pretty much tells me that I'm NOT female at all. If I were female, why wasn't I born with female genitalia? Sure, there are some intersexed people with ambiguous genitals, but I'm not at all intersexed. My chromosomes are the normal male XY, with absolutely no abnormalities.

The reality is that I'm male, and no amount of surgery changes that fact. I'm now four months post-op, and I've begun to transition to live as a male again. I feel it's the only way to be honest with myself and with society.

If you are considering this surgery, think very carefully about the consequences. Make sure that the doctor or counselor that's approving you for the surgery is qualified to evaluate whether you need the operation or not.

So many unnecessary operations of this type are carried out each year around the world, and in all too many cases, the effect is pain and regret, not only for the person who had the operation, but also for their families.

Awhile ago I watched a documentary on ABC about one man who regretted his surgery and was shocked by the gross inaccuracy of the statement the reporter used to introduce him: "Charles Kane is one of the few people in the world to change gender twice." [51] They had not done their homework. Even a little bit of research on their part would have shown that this isn't true. I have found more than a few regretters and I don't have the resources a massive powerful news organization like ABC has to find them.

2 In the next story we will see a story of regret that occurred only a year and a half after surgery, a painful reminder from a father who now finds himself without his genitalia and wanting to return to being a father again.

I am 46 and 1.5 years post op MTF. I struggled with my gender identity most of my life. I am so miserable and every day I struggle to get thru the next minute. I have to pray for the strength not to go to the gun store. Every minute is filled with suicidal thoughts. I can't live like this anymore. Please help me. Guide me what to do medically, surgically to fix this mess.

I am so glad I came across your website. After 10 months of post-op psychotherapy, I know sadly now my problems were great depression, unresolved issues as you said (I was sexually abused by my grandfather at 3 years old, father was killed in the line of duty when I was 5, grew up thinking I must be gay, had sex with men and was disgusted, and cross dressed most of my life.) My new therapist is

---

[51] ABC News' "Nightline", "My (Extra) Ordinary Family: My Kid Is Transgender", August 31, 2011,
http://abcnews.go.com/Nightline/video/charles-transregret-transgender-kids-sex-change-primetime-nightline-1442544

calling it a transvestic fetish that went terribly wrong, coupled with GID.

Why couldn't we get to this pre-op? It's just a sick money making industry as I see it. I have already removed the breast implants, and will be restarting testosterone soon. I am an airline pilot by trade; I have destroyed my career, my finances and my marriage and alienated my family.

The pain as you know is so great! It feels like a knife in my heart. I can't sleep. I pace the house looking in my shorts for my manhood. I am so disgusted with myself. How could a smart, successful guy get so lost? I had it all. Now I'm watching it slowly fade away. You and all the people that give me words of encouragement are the only thing keeping me going. I have rope, and I know when and where all the next guns shows are; I don't want to live like this. My therapist is going to recommend me to gender therapists; to get a surgical solution I can live with. At 46 years of age I just hope I have the strength to get there; my batteries are drained. I have not read your book; but I am willing to listen to your thoughts and ideas.

Have a good day. Thank you.

3 In this story from the UK[52] we read about a teenager who got caught up in the latest trend in gender change: starting the process at a much

---

[52] Katy Winter, "'I was born a boy, became a girl, and now I want to be a boy again': Britain's youngest sex swap patient to reverse her sex change treatment", *Daily Mail Sunday Mirror*, 29 October 2012, http://www.dailymail.co.uk/femail/article-2224753/Ria-Cooper-Britains-youngest-sex-change-patient-reverse-treatment.html#ixzz2LXcSu1bu

younger age, preferably before puberty, in an effort to find improved success. Many of us have seen the favorable publicity in the U.S. about children "needing" sex change treatment. But as this story demonstrates, regret can follow.

Ria Cooper made headlines last year when she became Britain's youngest sex change patient aged 17, after years of begging her family and the NHS to turn her in to a girl.

But now, having lived as a woman for less than a year the 18-year has decided to change back in to a man after suffering huge mental anguish as a woman.

Although Ms. Cooper underwent a thorough psychological assessment and counseling at Hull Royal Infirmary prior to starting her sex change therapy she has suffered such torment living as women that she has tried to commit suicide twice.

She told the Sunday Mirror: 'The hormones have made me feel up and down. One minute I feel moody and the next minute I feel really happy.'

'The night I tried to slash my wrists I'd downed a bottle of Jack Daniel's and just thought about how alone I am, and how my decision has alienated my family and how I will have to become a boy again to resolve it.'

This young person begged her family for years to allow her to become a girl, started the transition at age 17, and regretted it only one year later. She cancelled the operation that was scheduled and halted the hormone treatments.

She (or he) confirms the point I made in my book, *Paper Genders*. The brain hasn't matured enough to make this decision until the person reaches their mid-20s. So why would we encourage anyone in their teens or younger to undergo "treatments" with such long-term consequences?

Too quickly the diagnosis is made and we see the word "suicide" again is a constant companion of gender changers. This demonstrates the sad truth: it is not "happily ever after."

4 The story of Alan Finch, featured on an ABC documentary on Australian television, is full of twists and turns that never seem to end. Born a male, but confused about his sexuality as a teenager, Alan identified as a transsexual at age 19. In a decision supported by health-care professionals, Alan underwent sex change surgery at 21 and became Helen Finch. He (she) married a man, then divorced and became a man again. By the age of 30, Alan returned to his birth gender. This kind of journey is so painful and so unnecessary.

Alan had been misdiagnosed with gender identity disorder. He now understands what he needed was simple psychotherapy, not sex change surgery. If you are interested, you can watch the Australian documentary called *Boy Interrupted*, seen on *Australian Story*. [53]

5 This next person emailed me his firsthand impressions of the transition process in both the U.S. and the UK. I think it could be helpful for us to consider:

---

[53] ABC, *Australian Story*, September 1, 2003, available at www.abc.net.au/austory/archives2003.htm.

Many friends have said I am transsexual in that they think I am more female than male, and they may have a point. However - and this is the main point - I do not see myself as a woman and would never consider surgery. I came to this conclusion many years ago. I often imagine myself as woman though and love wearing the clothes and making up - and even doing what I think are female things - BUT the moment I look at real women reality hits - it's a very sharp reminder - if you have the courage to admit it to yourself.

I have seen many transitions and go through the surgery and say how happy they are, but they can't get jobs, they lose their families yet they still say they are happy! The only TS [transsexual] I know whose transition was justified to me was one who was born sexually ambiguous and forced to live as a man by his father. When his father died he became a woman, which he really was in the first place, and is truly happy.

In Canada, Europe and the UK, to get SRS [sex reassignment surgery] free on the health service you have to live as a woman for a year, and be seen to integrate successfully into female society. You also have to support yourself economically in the same period and show yourself not to be a potential drain on society. You come under the supervision of a real psychologist for that time and he/she will assess you not only for readiness and commitment but also whether other factors are present such as depression, bi-polar that could skew the assessment. There are good reasons for failure.

This really works - there was a TV program in the UK where a transsexual was followed by the cameras throughout his year. It was rough and the man had to face up to a reality pretty quickly. The psychologist's bar was very high.

In the U.S. nothing like this happens. The transgender goes to a support group who convinces him that he is a transgender and tells *him what he wants to hear. He goes to a local counselor (usually no more than a Social Worker) who tells him he's transsexual and should have the operation and gives him sessions (which he pays for) to convince him he's ready. At no point is a psychologist involved or anyone who is willing to tell him what he doesn't want to hear - that he is mostly delusional and needs to sort out other issues first. I am convinced that most transgenders have other issues going on as well as their cross-dressing.*

I have told many transgenders in the U.S. about the year in Europe and the UK only to have it, and me, very aggressively ridiculed, which tells its own story.

Thank you I hope it helps.

6 The last in the six stories of regret shows that my efforts to get the word out about regret are worthwhile. Sparing even one person from an unnecessary sex change is reward for the work.

Walt,

I really appreciate you speaking about this issue. I have struggled for most of my life with gender identity issues, and often wish I were a girl.

I am a cross-dresser, who is recently divorced, and I thought this was my opportunity to change my sex. I have been doing quite a lot of research and stumbled across your YouTube videos, as well as some others.

I now realize I have a gender fetish, but I would be unhappy to change my sex and then regret it. I haven't read your book, but what your (and others) videos say have touched my life. I now just hope and pray I can find a way to accept myself for who I am. For whatever reason, I have been put in this body with this fetish, and I need to learn to cope and not dwell on what could be.

I thank you again for helping me to not make a life altering change that is irreversible".

Diagnosing gender issues requires a sound therapist and steady slow talk therapy to prevent letters like we saw in these six stories of regret.

The controversy about changing genders will not end. Not with this book, not with a 41% suicide attempt rate, not from publishing a multitude of true stories of wasted years spent on "male to female and back" or the other way around. No, the unnecessary gender surgeries will not stop.

We can hope to prevent some suicides by improving the diagnosis of disorders that cause the desire to change gender and by providing ongoing psychological treatment. But we have a long way to go before we will see the medical and activist communities care about suicides and regret among transgenders and encourage full discussion and disclosure of the serious issues.

Decades of Suicide

9

"I never saw a successful patient.
For the most part they remained misfits."
—Dr. John Hoopes, former Johns Hopkins Gender Identity
Clinic Chairman [54]

The first reported sex change surgeries in the U.S. were done over 40 years ago. You would think after all this time the controversy would long be over but the science is all over the place in its conclusions. Early on, studies that reported poor outcomes were lambasted as inaccurate, but now we are beginning to see they were quite accurate.

The gender change power groups always report that great success has come to all who suffer with gender issues and

---

[54] Laura Wexler, "Identity Crisis," Style Magazine, *The Baltimore Sun*, January/February 2007, downloaded on Feb. 23, 2013 from http://www.baltimorestyle.com/index.php/style/features_article/fe_sexchange_jf07/

undergo surgical transformation. But the suicide statistics tell a very different story. The advocate Transgender Task Force group themselves broadcast the consequences of changing genders in survey results published in 2011.[55] They say transgenders face discrimination, anti-transgender bias and structural racism, live in poverty more than the general population and a *staggering 41% reported attempting suicide.* Even with results like this they take great pride and boast the gender surgery is highly successful in improving transgender lives. Really?

The attempted suicide rate among transgenders is 41% and the actual rate of death by suicide is estimated by one source to between 31% and 50%.[56] This is not a story of success. How can it be called successful when one-third to one-half of gender changers commits suicide? From my vantage point, success is just a word, not an objective finding.

It makes me uncomfortable having witnessed more than 40 years of gender madness powered by advocate political groups more and more becoming a malignant cancer as it overtakes society. Yes, it is uncomfortable to consider that political power groups are like a malignant cancer in that the result is deadly and it destroys the very foundation of family, sadly.

---

[55] Grant, Jaime M., et. al., *Injustice at Every Turn: A Report of the National Transgender Discrimination Survey.* op. cit.

[56] Laura's Playground, "Transgender Suicide Report: Actual," downloaded on June 5, 2013, from http://www.lauras-playground.com/transgender_suicide_report.htm

I'm guilty because I fell for this nonsense of surgical genders. My family would have been much better off made up of a real man and a real woman, not a real woman and a man made into a surgical facsimile of a woman.

90% LOST TO FOLLOW UP

We will look for some reason why they report success when the suicide attempts and suicide deaths are so high. One big clue can be found in chapter 5 of a huge text book titled *Principles of Transgender Medicine and Surgery*:

> Several factors complicate efforts to systematically study the long-term effects of gender reassignment surgery. First, a large proportion of the patients (up to 90 percent) are lost to follow-up. [57]

Ninety percent are lost to follow-up? So that means as few as ten percent of the patient population can be found and included in follow-up findings. With the loss of a whopping 90% of transgenders unable to participate in the study results, it would be intellectually dishonest to say that studies prove surgery is successful. They arrive at the conclusion "gender changing is successful" based on a small percent of transgenders. It is not even a random sample, but simply those who could be found and consented to be interviewed. In my view it would stand to reason that when a large proportion of the patients are lost to

---

[57] Ettner, R., Monstrey, S., Eyler, A.E., *Principles of Transgender Medicine and Surgery*, Haworth Press Human Sexuality Series, Taylor & Francis, 2007, Chapter 5: Surgery: general principles by Stan Monstrey, Griet De Cuypere, Randi Ettner, p. 96

follow-up, using the remaining sample cannot lead to sound research conclusions.

While the transgender political power groups argue forcefully for easy-to-get gender surgery, maverick transgenders like me are asking for much more caution prior to surgery. I suggest medical protocol needs to require a much better job of screening to uncover comorbid disorders.

Research studies published over 40 years ago show that some considered the idea of looking for secondary psychological disorders but the homosexual power groups discouraged the practice. So you have controversy and conflicting agendas: the powerful gender change pushers on one side and on the other side, individuals who take notice of the broken lives and deaths, and scrutinize the research for its scientifically factual basis and see success is limited.

Why have I chosen to lock my focus squarely on prevalence of suicide? I consciously made this choice out of concern for transgenders and those who love them. In my view, the suicide rate illustrates how the surgery fails at least one out of three people. But that is simply the starting point for counting failure.

Start with thirty percent, the low estimate on the transgender suicide prevention website; then add in those who have medical-surgical complications, those who were diagnosed incorrectly, those who fail in their social and economic adjustment, and those who revert to their original birth gender. What about those transgenders who suffer from alcoholism, drug addiction and prostitution? Shall we include them as well?

I start to think it might add up to the ninety percent who could not be found for the long term studies. Perhaps the ten percent who are readily found are the stories of success. But sadly, about the lost ninety percent we will never know.

EARLY HOPKINS CONTROVERSY

The controversies about sex change surgery are not new. In 1966 with the first reported gender sex surgery performed in the U.S. at Johns Hopkins in their new Gender Identity Clinic (GIC), controversy started and remains to dog the procedure today. A feature article in the Sunday edition of the *Baltimore Sun* in 2007 by Laura Wexler provides interesting insights into those early days. Back then the controversy was inside the walls of Johns Hopkins.

In 1965, when Johns Hopkins became the first hospital in the nation to formally establish a sex change program, it shocked the nation. It also created a lab in which theories about nature vs. nurture— and body vs. mind— clashed in fascinating and ferocious ways. Four decades later, the implications are still being felt.

Given the uncertainty [about how to assess who should get surgery], at the clinic's monthly meetings the psychiatrists frequently chose to err on the side of wait-and-see, recommending therapy instead of advancing a patient onto the next stage of the process. That often set them in direct opposition to Money, as GIC chairman Hoopes recalls. "John Money would argue very forcefully that someone was a candidate ... that he knew the patient very well and if this program was going to make any headway this patient should be accepted," he says. [58]

---

[58] Laura Wexler, "Identity Crisis," op. cit.

Money seemed to be concerned about furthering an agenda rather than caring about the welfare of the patients. The patients, too, were insistent on their need for surgery:

...The patients didn't want to see a psychiatrist. To see one inferred they had mental problems," says one psychiatrist member of the GIC who did not wish to be quoted by name. "They took exception."

The patients' conviction that surgery—not therapy—was the only thing that could end their suffering is still a prominent theme of sufferers today. Back then, patients would read medical journals to learn how to present themselves to the Johns Hopkins medical committee in order to qualify for surgery. Today, the internet is awash with information on where to go and how to get surgery, and the surgeons are only too happy to oblige the patients who line up with their fistfuls of dollars.

Some of the early supporters of the procedure changed their viewpoint as the evidence began to mount. GIC Chairman Hoopes originally was a proponent of the gender surgery as treatment, but with the benefit of hindsight in the 2007 *Baltimore Sun* article he is quoted as saying: "I never saw a successful patient. For the most part they remained misfits."

Dr. Jon Meyer, who succeeded Hoopes as head of the Hopkins GIC, conducted a major study of the Hopkins GIC patients that sought to measure objectively the benefits of gender surgery over the long term. He announced his results in 1979. According to Laura Wexler's article:

"To say that this type of surgery cures psychiatric disturbance is incorrect. We now

have objective evidence that there is no real difference in the transsexual's adjustment to life in terms of jobs, educational attainment, marital adjustment and social stability," he [Meyer] said. He later told The New York Times, "My personal feeling is that surgery is not a proper treatment for a psychiatric disorder, and it's clear to me that these patients have severe psychological problems that don't go away following surgery."
59

It has been decades since they criticized Meyer's 1979 report but he was correct then and it remains true today. Transgenders remain psychologically-troubled misfits. I received the following note from a transgender who has been working and living as a female for ten years. It demonstrates how correct Dr. Jon Meyer was in his assessment of the failure of gender surgery.

I underwent surgery about 10 years ago. I was convinced it was the right thing to do—regrettably, it was not. The price I paid was dear; I hurt the ones I loved the most—my children, my siblings, my parents, and my partner.

By all appearances I am a success story. I have a good job as a high school teacher, I live stealth, have had a fairly active love life, etc., but none of this can ever make up for the pain and guilt I feel everyday of my life. As accepting as my son has been, every time I look at him I see the hurt in his eyes. I can feel his sense of loss over his father, and it tears at my very soul.

---

59 Laura Wexler, "Identity Crisis," op. cit.

Believe it or not, I have even gone to a therapist and several surgeons—with little success. I just get told it's a normal part of the "adjustment phase" (an awfully long phase!!!). They say, "You make a nice woman—be happy!" But I'm not happy!

I am wondering if you know of any surgeon that will remove my breast implants. I really would like to start living as a man again.

I myself had a dissociative disorder which was undiagnosed. The recommended treatment for my distress was to cut my genitals off and declare I was now the female, Laura Jensen. I now know with absolute certainty it was my troubled mind that needed fixing, not the removal of body parts, a barbaric and completely unnecessary surgical treatment.

THE REAL REGRET NUMBER

Years ago studies in America and Holland suggested around one in twenty post-operative transsexuals changes his or her mind after surgery, and around one in ten never adjusts and often becomes deeply depressed.

Any time I discover a study that includes the ninety percent lost to follow-up; I stand up and take notice (and cheer). A study from Sweden released in 2011 included every transgender who underwent surgery there from 1973-2003. Their objective was to estimate mortality, morbidity, and criminal rate after surgical sex reassignment of transsexual persons. It is like an echo from the past and proof Dr. Jon Meyer was correct in his assessment in studying the Hopkins Gender Identity Clinic patients so many years ago. Their conclusion is that persons with transsexualism, after sex reassignment, have considerably higher risks for mortality, suicidal behavior, and psychiatric morbidity than the general population. [60]

Troubled minds need care. The end result of ignoring transgenders' psychological issues? Lives unnecessarily cut short, families torn to shreds, and a life on the dole for many who survive. Their lives are a mess as much after surgery as they were prior to the gender change surgery. They remain misfits. In my own life I have found that even thirty years post-surgery, I will always feel the hurt due to the pain I inflicted on my kids.

When the option for gender surgery started so many years ago, it was we adults with gender issues who were the willing participants. Today our kids are targeted by the homosexual and transgender power groups. Take a look at this letter I received from a mother in March of 2013. She wanted to report to me what is now troubling her:

My son is in high school and I have seen posters in hallways saying that all students support the rights of gays by wearing certain colors. The world is changing so fast and most people are clueless. My daughter, now in 8th grade, says that many kids now call themselves "bisexual." This is a scary time to be a young person.

Sodomy is celebrated and heterosexual boys and girls feel the pressure to call themselves bisexual just to be hip. This is a scary time to be a young person and a scary time to be a young person with gender issues.

---

[60] Dhejne C, Lichtenstein P, et. al., op. cit.

Megalomaniac Docs

10

Megalomania—a condition characterized by delusional fantasies of wealth, power, or omnipotence; an obsession with grandiose or extravagant things or actions.[61]

Sounds to me like megalomaniac is the perfect depiction of the doctor at a children's hospital who wants to change little boys into little girls. If that sounds sick, that is because it is. I want to tell them, "Go find a cure for cancer and leave the children alone to mature as they were made."

Let's face it: kids are vulnerable to the power of doctors. They and their parents are easy targets. They can be manipulated into trying "experimental" treatments, such as hormone blocking drugs, "Experimental" is the right word.

---

[61] megalomania. Dictionary.com. *The American Heritage® Stedman's Medical Dictionary*. Houghton Mifflin Company. http://dictionary.reference.com/ browse/megalomania (accessed: February 26, 2013).

Neither the doctor nor the child has any possible way of knowing the objective long-term consequences. The treatment is intended to interrupt the process of puberty through injections of drugs that block the production of gender hormones. Personally, from the results I see, I think this should be considered child abuse.

The gender changing doctors have extraordinary support from the very powerful, well-financed activists who have their own agenda for pushing kids toward gender change. These damn doctors start thinking they are God, because, after all, they can intervene and change a child's God-given gender sex. This feeling of power is addicting and they will never admit they are wrong. It becomes an obsession, such that they see a gender change in every kid in order to feed their self-aggrandizement. I might even suggest that the megalomaniac doctors themselves have psychopathological disorders and use their power to manipulate vulnerable and depressed young kids in order to build their reputation in the transgender medical world.

The doctors do not suffer the consequences when the treatment goes wrong. The stories of kids entering into such psychologically destructive treatment read like horror fiction. In a typical scenario, the doctor refers the child to a psychologist who is more like the "closer" for the deal, similar to buying a car. The diagnosis is subjective and approval of the treatment was a forgone conclusion.

We are bombarded today—transgenders are cropping up everywhere. It has become complete transgender madness in public schools from coast to coast. You would think every last kid who questions his self image is a transgender. According to a study at University of California Los Angeles, an estimated 0.3% of adults in the U.S. are transgender, about 680,000 people.[62]

The National Survey on Drug Use and Health reported in 2008 that 8.3% of adolescents (an estimated 2 million aged 12-17) experienced at least one major depressive episode.[63] The survey says the signs exhibited by depressed adolescents include problems with self image and talk of suicide. Kids who feel they are the wrong gender express difficulty with their self image and talk of suicide. This in my view becomes potentially deadly when the child comes into the lair of a gender specialist wielding hormone blocking gender treatments. I say, "Treat them for depression and stop suggesting they need to change their birth gender!"

With the megalomaniac doctors' rush to change genders in children, and no long-term studies available to discourage the practice, we can forecast the continued accumulation of stories of regret and sadness.

---

[62] Gary J. Gates, "How many people are lesbian, gay, bisexual, and transgender?", The Williams Institute, UCLA School of Law, April, 2011, downloaded on June 17, 2013, as http://williamsinstitute.law.ucla.edu/wp-content/uploads/Gates-How-Many-People-LGBT-Apr-2011.pdf

[63] Substance Abuse and Mental Health Services Administration. (2009), *Results from the 2008 National Survey on Drug Use and Health: National Findings* (Office of Applied Studies, NSDUH Series H-36, HHS Publication No. SMA 09-4434). Rockville, MD., http://www.samhsa.gov/data/2k8/youthdepress /youthdepress.htm (accessed March 16, 2013)

Let's look again at the story told in a previous chapter, '*I was born a boy, became a girl, and now I want to be a boy again': Britain's youngest sex swap patient to reverse her sex change* to see the result of a child making the decision to change genders at age 16 or 17. This narrative illustrates why I call this treatment child abuse, or more precisely in this case, teen abuse. To irreversibly take a young person with his entire life ahead of him and experiment, altering his body is pure abuse. This confirms my assertions that gender change ends up in regret and even reversion back to the birth gender.

> Ria Cooper made headlines last year when she became Britain's youngest sex change patient aged 17, after years of begging her family and the NHS to turn her in to a girl.
>
> But now, having lived as a woman for less than a year the 18-year has decided to change back in to a man after suffering huge mental anguish as a woman.
>
> She has cancelled the full sex change operation that was scheduled for January and ceased the female hormone therapy that has seen her develop breasts saying that she has found the changes overwhelming and that they have made her deeply unhappy. [64]

In case you are wondering if this person followed the Standards of Care, yes, British medical professionals provided a thorough psychological assessment and counseling prior to starting the

---

[64] Winter, Katy, *Daily Mail*, op. cit.

child down this path. We can see how ineffective that was—it failed to protect the child—and Britain's protocol is more rigid than that of the U.S.

The advocates for hormone blocker treatment for adolescents say they are harmless and the effects are reversible. This young person's story, like so many of the examples and research I have provided throughout this book, show that risk of suicide is always present. Ms. Ria Cooper says in her own words,

> "The night I tried to slash my wrists I'd downed a bottle of Jack Daniel's and just thought about how alone I am, and how my decision has alienated my family and how I will have to become a boy again to resolve it."

Attempted suicide. Harmless? Reversible? The megalomaniac doctors ignore the very real, harmful and irreversible psychological effects on the children and the risk of suicide that result from their playing God with children's lives.

The advocates see Ms. Cooper's suicide attempt and blame the family for making the young person feel alienated. No self-reflection by the advocates occurs, nor any by the doctor or the psychologist. Everything in her process followed the current Standards of Care yet failure came quickly, and was almost followed by the deadly result of suicide. Who ends up with the consequences that result from the failure? Not the doctor. Not the psychologist. Only the 18 year old who was born a boy and his family.

Should we even consider radical gender change treatment for a kid at the request of mom, dad or the kid? The activist doctors would say that patient outcomes are better if the gender change is started before puberty begins changing the body.

Every step in the process has irreversible effects on the child. Delaying puberty with hormone blockers: Don't think for a moment that this won't have an emotional impact on the child that will last a lifetime. Next step: injections of cross-gender hormone therapy which causes lifetime infertility. And lastly, surgery on the genitals. Talk about irreversible effects!

Does a teen have the ability to plan for and foresee the consequences of his or her actions? Anyone who has been around a teenager for any length of time knows the answer. The answer is an emphatic NO—a child cannot make such a drastic life decision. The brain is not mature or developed until the age of 20 or older to understand such consequences.[65]

The megalomaniac doctors, acting as if they were God with our young kids' lives when research says, "No, the brain is much too young," should have their medical license revoked. Placing kids at risk when they know a child's brain is not developed enough to make an informed decision to enter into gender and sex change therapies is flat out child abuse.

Says Dr. Jay Giedd of the National Institute of Mental Health: "Teens are capable of enormous intellectual and artistic accomplishments. But that basic part of the brain that gives us

---

[65] Heyer, Walt, *Paper Genders*, Make Waves Publishing, 2011, p.51

strategies and organizing and perhaps warns us of potential consequences isn't fully on board yet." [66]

Dr. Andrew Garner of the American Academy of Pediatrics notes that the adolescent brain has not reached full maturity until the age of 24. Yes, not until the age of 24.

What about using hormone blockers, as the advocates claim, doesn't that buy time to make the decision? After all, Dr. Spack of Boston Children's Hospital recommends hormone blockers for pre-teen kids with gender confusion. The sole purpose is to delay the onset of puberty and its production of testosterone or estrogen on pre-teen kids. But I say that this sets in motion a false idea within the child's psyche such as "I will become a new boy (or girl)" when the reality is they will always be transgender.

For the pre-teen the gender change looks like a fun ride at Disney World but in all likelihood it will end up in a nightmare, a nightmare that can lead to suicide or attempted suicide.

The megalomaniac doctor who acts all powerful over God is making fools of us all. Just because they can change the child's outer appearance doesn't mean the result of the treatments is a different gender. It sets the child up for an adulthood of perpetual make-believe. Treating undeveloped kids in the cruel and inhumane practice of misrepresenting the outcome of treatment, saying it will result in a different gender is, in fact, medical malpractice. I feel much more oversight and risk of loss of medical credentials in the U.S. must be assessed

---

[66] Ibid., p.52

against doctors who take such risks, especially in the use of hormone blockers with children.

Child gender doctors like Dr. Spack focus on treating the gender anxiety by delaying puberty with hormone blockers. They assume this treatment will also resolve the depression. The research, however, shows that depression disorders usually have no single cause and therefore also have no single treatment.[67] By promoting puberty blocking treatments, Dr. Spack is not directly addressing other possible factors for the child's depression, such as abuse, neglect and psychiatric issues.

I know of many boy-to-girl transgenders who were adorned with make-up, nail polish and girl's clothing, sometimes by mom, other times by one or more sisters, or like me, by a misguided grandmother. Some secretly cross-dressed in their sister's or mother's clothing and found the behavior exciting and stimulating like a drug and became addicted to the risk and excitement. Cross-dressing can lead to gender anxiety and depression—I can provide testimony to that as truth.

Parents must keep in mind that for the advocate doctor it is all upside and no risk at all for doctor. But it is a very different story for a child. All unintended long term downside consequences for the unnecessary treatment fall squarely on the child, even after you are long gone. Parents are either vulnerable to the power of a doctor or they go down the path of gender change with their child in the misguided hope that it will help them. Personally, from the results I see, I think this practice should be considered a punishable crime.

---

[67] Winter, Katy, op. cit.

The casual dismissal of comorbid disorders by doctors who treat gender discomfort of people at any age is a reckless disregard for the known and well-documented depression and anxiety disorders that, if left untreated over time, become a leading cause of suicide.

A systemic problem in the treatment of gender dysphoria is that all who suggest they need a gender change are led to the slaughter, no matter how distressing their life issues, current or past. The gender change advocates seize every opportunity to advance the agenda, and show no concern for providing effective care.

There is no proof transgenders are born. How a child acts out their gender role will vary depending on the parent or parents, siblings and anyone else who has an active role spending time with the child from a very young age.[68] Researchers are looking into the influences of early childhood and gender development.

Susan Witt, Ph.D., Professor of Child Development at the University of Akron writes:

> As children move through childhood and into adolescence, they are exposed to many factors which influence their attitudes and behaviors regarding gender roles. These attitude and behaviors are generally learned first in the home and reinforced by the child's peers, school experiences, and television viewing. However the strongest influence on gender role

---

[68] Heyer, Walt, *Paper Genders*, Make Waves Publishing, 2011, p. 55

development seems to occur within the family setting, with parents passing on, both overtly and covertly, to their children their own beliefs about gender.[69]

Researchers and professors alike agree the way parents interact or don't interact in the baby's early years is how their brain becomes hard wired as it matures and grows. As the new baby interacts with their environment, their brain is developing pathways for visual stimulation, sounds, and emotions expressed by others such as shouting, crying, anger, or spanking. The baby's brain will become hard wired, that is, their view of the world gets shaped through early experiences.

Those cumulative experiences of childhood can lead to depressive and anxiety disorders and a skewed perception of gender. In some people, depression and anxiety become part of the complex gender hard wiring. Add in a culture of sweeping transgender activism in schools and on the internet and the result can be a child or adult that put their hope on gender change as the answer to their confusion and angst.

The problem is the parents encourage the megalomaniac doctors who do not formulate a treatment plan that explores the underlying complexities and give hope of a normal life. Instead they revel in the opportunity to play God, while adding one more person to the suicide watch list.

---

[69] Susan D. Witt, PhD , "Parental Influence on Children's Socialization to Gender Roles," *Adolescence*, Summer, 1997, downloaded from http://gozips.uakron.edu/~susan8/parinf.htm

WHAT ABOUT PARENTS?

When the activists say gender issues originate in the womb think "family dynamics" instead. If you or you know someone who is struggling with gender issues you need to know the following.

It is possible for nonconforming people to evolve into gender dysphoria over time. They need to explore the onset of their gender discomfort and consider that perhaps the home environment lacked adequate gender modeling.

The treatment process should not involve a change in birth gender expression or body modifications. Medical treatments which start with hormone therapy most often will escalate to gender dysphoria when it perhaps does not exist. In my own experience this was true.

Parents perhaps contribute to childhood gender nonconformity and narcissistic development. The development of the child's self identification can be influenced by excessive focus on the child's looks, behaviors and gender change suggestions. Do not underestimate the parental influence. If a parent widely supports gender diversity, the child may seek to change genders as a way to gain control over the parent and to prevent rules from being applied to them. In my previous book, *Paper Genders,* I documented how transsexualism stemmed from early family dynamics. Research says narcissism likely has links to family dynamics as well.[70]

---

[70] MayoClinic.com, http://www.mayoclinic.com/health/narcissistic-personality-disorder/DS00652/DSECTION=causes

My concern is how we have made our kids think birth gender is irrelevant. In our schools where peer pressure has always been great, we make it even more stressful by allowing children to switch genders at school. Massachusetts is allowing kids to change genders "at will" in school, boys using the girl's bathroom and girls using the boy's bathroom, as you can see in this news piece:

> Last week the Massachusetts Department of Education issued directives for handling transgender students – including allowing them to use the bathrooms of their choice or to play on sports teams that correspond to the gender with which they identify.
>
> The 11-page directive also urged schools to eliminate gender-based clothing and gender-based activities – like having boys and girls line up separately to leave the classroom.
>
> Schools will now be required to accept a student's gender identity on face value.
>
> The new rules would also prevent teachers and administrators from telling parents with which gender their child identifies.[71]

The lawmakers making open gender laws for schools are placing a bull's eye squarely on the back of the gender non-

---

[71] Starnes, Todd, "Students Who Refuse to Affirm Transgender Classmates Face Punishment", February 20, 2013, FoxNews Radio, downloaded on June 15, 2013, from http://radio.foxnews.com/toddstarnes/top-stories/students-who-refuse-to-affirm-transgender-classmates-face-punishment.html

compliant kids. They place kids at an elevated risk of harassment, bullying, vulgar talk and even suicide. The heckling and bullying that will occur off the school grounds will be unbearable for some. Allowing this complete nonsense will no doubt elevate suicide rates.

The cowardly lawmakers sit with armed guards just outside their doors. They should be ashamed and held accountable for every single young gender non-compliant person who commits suicide. The lawmakers should be required by law to attend each of their funerals.

My grandmother apparently enjoyed cross-dressing me in girls clothing when I was only about five years of age. Now I look back on this early childhood experience as the onset of my life-long struggle with gender dysphoria, which developed into a dissociative disorder that took decades to resolve. Cross-dressing a child perhaps looks harmless. No one can foresee what devastating consequences can occur when you introduce cross-dressing into a young child's routine experience. If I can serve as evidence, let me warn you: it is risky and need not ever happen.

Parents need to deliberately reinforce the child's birth gender and not fall prey to the current day *transgender gender*. Some parents will support their children's desire to gender cross-dress. When they do, we need to question their ability to be a parent.

The LGBT has influenced schools to sponsor events that encourage children to challenge gender norms with "transgender day" and "gay pride day." These events are a misguided attempt to help troubled children feel included. But it all elevates the risk of teen suicides because of the peer pressure to "go along with it." The message to kids who are troubled or confused by their gender or sexuality is: Too bad; you're stuck with it. No help is available.

I'm blowing the whistle on how it feels to be taken down the wrong path into the depths of the transgender experience. Now let's look at some studies about transgenderism that will blow the whistle on the activists and blow your mind.

Walt's Blog

11

There is no female brain in the wrong male body.
Current studies do not support the transsexual condition.
Nor do they support the Harry Benjamin Syndrome.
–From a whistleblower physician

Many in the transgender community have undergone hormone treatment and/or genital surgery based on theories about the transgender diagnosis only to find out now that they have been living their lives based on lies. Many of them write to me to express extreme anger at the transgender establishment for feeding them theories as if it were truth.

With help from a physician who generously shares his wisdom and insight with me, I've blogged about transgender theories and the studies that debunk them.

What happens when a doctor who until recently advocated for gender transition as necessary evaluates the current research with an objective eye? He discovers that there is no such thing as transsexual.

What I love about this physician's viewpoint is that he has the education and training to take the various theories that have been bandied about concerning the origins of transgenderism and show how the latest research findings totally and irrefutably discredit them.

These blog postings originally appeared on *Sex Change Info* at waltheyer.com.

04/30/2013

Physician says,
"We have willfully failed"

In his startling whistleblower-type letters to me in April 2013 a physician speaks out:

Any physician worthy of his degree must treat ONLY with the Hippocratic Oath. First do no harm. In this regard, we have willfully failed.

-- There is no female brain in the wrong male body

-- Current studies do not support the transsexual condition

-- Nor do the current studies support the Harry Benjamin Syndrome.

Please don't mention my name. You would be surprised at the hostility of transsexual persons against physicians. I really do think that lots of physicians are very intimidated by them. The patients use the physicians and the physicians use the patients. It is deplorable.

This physician tells me after many years of actively writing articles to support the need for surgery he now has great concerns, as he admits, "We have failed those with gender identity problems miserably."

The doctor wants me to report several things you need to know:

A study of 1986 [1] disproved all of the other studies that suggested that H-Y antigen caused transsexualism.

The 2013 Rome study and the 2009 Japan study reported in my blog on April 6th, 2013, disproved any alterations in the DNA of the main sex determining genes in transsexuals, proving transgenders are normal males, not a smidgeon of abnormality exists in the genetic make-up of transgenders. The males are normal. We now know gender issues are psychosocial or psychological, and perhaps psychiatric issues exist in transgenders which manifest in gender identity issues. The staggering suicide rates are evidence that changing genders is causing harm.

The doctor says,

"Walt, I agree with you. We should have seen this disaster in the making. Here is a link to an article from 1979 with quotes from Harry Benjamin's colleague, Dr. Charles Ihlenfeld:

Among the reasons for exercising extreme care in giving hormones, according to Ihlenfeld, is the fact that 80 percent of the patients who want to change their sex shouldn't do it. "There is too much unhappiness among people who have had the surgery," he said. "Too many of them end as suicides." [2]

I'm grateful this physician stepped forward and I hope more are willing to talk about the failure of gender surgery.

Walt Heyer, the Maverick Transgender
www.sexchangeregret.com

References:

[1] Stephen Wachtel Ph.D., Richard Green M.D., Neal G. Simon Ph.D., Alison Reichart, Linda Cahill, John Hall, Dean Nakamura, Gwendolyn Wachtel, Walter Futterweit M.D., Stanley H. Biber M.D., Charles Ihlenfeld M.D., "On the expression of H-Y antigen in transsexuals", Archives of Sexual Behavior, February 1986, Volume 15, Issue 1, pp 51-68, http://link.springer.com/article/ 10.1007%2FBF01542304? LI=true#page-1

[2] Garrett Oppenheim, Ph.D., "Ihlenfeld Cautions on Hormones", Transition, No. 8 - January/February 1979 Copyright 1979 - Transition/ Source: J2CP Information Services, http://lvtgw.jadephoenix.org/Info_htm/Herbal_G/ginko_b2.htm

The studies in the next blog entry say that "transgender" is a symptom found in a wide range of mental disorders. Gender change will not resolve it.

05/06/2013

4 Studies Say It's Mental Disorders

Perhaps it's time to pound the drums more loudly than ever about what I think as the greatest medical fraud in our nation's history. 30% of transgenders commit suicide because their mental disorders remain undiagnosed, and as such will not be treated.

I have long held that individuals who suffer from gender distress have one of a handful of unresolved mental illnesses that exists side by side with their gender stress. The gender distress is not acting alone but binds with an additional comorbid mental illness. "We found 90% of these diverse patients had at least one other significant form of "psychopathology" says a study reported in 2009 by the Department of Psychiatry, Case Western Reserve University, Cleveland, Ohio. The psychopathologies they found in their study were "mood and anxiety regulation and adaptation in the world". (1)

Everywhere we see the constant rhetoric about gender change success and yet not one sound media report that acknowledges 30% of transgenders commit suicide because of untreated mental illness.

Suicide.org states that 90% of all suicides are the direct result of untreated mental illness.

What other treatment focuses on surgery while 30% of the patients commit suicide?

The professional people and media rigorously maintain "political correctness." Most of the voices and media blindly talk about the long-term value of a gender transition and hormones treatments, suggesting transgenders lives are improved when the truth is, their lives are often worse because of their untreated mental illness evidenced by their 30% suicide rate. The surgery has failed to resolve the gender distress and often elevates their anxiety and depression.

You can see for yourself. The aforementioned study from Case Western Reserve University raises concern about those who care for transgendered adults and the media for spinning rhetoric that transsexualism is a civil rights issue. Concern because they do not disclose that nearly 90% of the time transgenders suffer serious mental issues, disorders that are causing their regret and premature deaths. An ongoing mental health issue, for sure.

As a transgender I do not feel transgenders have a legitimate civil rights issue but do have a legitimate mental health concern. If in fact we want to prevent their suicides we need to focus on the issues of suicides. Making transgenders a civil rights issue will not reduce suicides.

Studies from Sweden [2] and the Netherlands [3] showed 90% of transgenders have mental disorders consisting of depression and anxiety—known causes of suicide. These studies provide irrefutable evidence transgenders overwhelmingly suffer from untreated mental disorders. Gender surgery is not the required treatment for depression and anxiety or other transgender mental disorders.

A 2013 study of anxiety and depression in transgender individuals showed the rates of depression and anxiety for those in the study far surpassed the rates in the general population. [4]

But if the professionals who treat transgenders remain unwilling to focus on and treat the mental disorders nothing will change in their diagnosis or treatment. If insanity is doing the same thing over and over again expecting different results, who is insane here?

I'm not a doctor or a psychologist, but if I can see the overwhelming evidence showing that mental illness is behind gender stress, shouldn't the medical professionals see it?

Insanity is to focus on XY and XX patterns, hormone treatments and surgery or born in the wrong body, when it's mental illness.

References:

1. Levine SB, Solomon A., "Meanings and political implications of 'psychopathology' in a gender identity clinic: a report of 10 cases", Department of Psychiatry, Case Western Reserve University, Cleveland, Ohio, USA, J Sex Marital Ther. 2009;35(1):40-57.
http://www.ncbi.nlm.nih.gov/ pubmed/19105079

2. Dhejne C, Lichtenstein P, "Long-term follow-up of transsexual persons undergoing sex reassignment surgery: cohort study in Sweden", op. cit.
http://www.ncbi.nlm.nih.gov/pubmed/21364939

3. Joost à Campo, M.D. et. al., "Psychiatric Comorbidity of Gender Identity Disorders: A Survey Among Dutch Psychiatrists, op. cit.
http://ajp.psychiatryonline.org/article.aspx?articleID=176330

4. Budge SL, Adelson JL, Howard KA ,"Anxiety and depression in transgender individuals: The roles of transition status, loss, social support, and coping", J Consult Clin Psychol. 2013 Jun;81(3):545-57. Epub 2013 Feb 11.
http://www.ncbi.nlm.nih.gov/pubmed/23398495

Walt Heyer, the Maverick Transgender
www.sexchangeregret.com

05/16/2013

Sex Change Rip-off:
a Bogus Procedure

I wonder how many of us would have chosen the surgery if:

- Surgeons had the courage to tell us the truth (your gender will not change) and

– The legal system was willing to be factual and tell the transgender: "Your gender will not change, although cosmetically you may look like it has."

We transgenders have been lied to all these years. Doctors and surgeons have been ripping us off because they told us we indeed would be changed from a man into a real woman after the gender change surgery. However, the surgery only castrates the male but even at that you can get a change to a phony birth record.

I have a message for those surgeons and doctors:

You have caused untold amounts of post-ops to commit suicide by selling a phony gender change.

The deaths, the regret, the reversal surgeries and lies need to stop. The suicides should be investigated as a crime by surgeons against people with untreated mental illness and research studies have proven that to be true.

I want to prevent suicides. The Dr. Ihlenfeld report stated thirty years ago that 80% should not transition. The transgender sex change is a rip-off because:

1. The gender reassignment surgery will not change anyone from a male to a female or female to a male.
2. They are operating on good people who have not been properly evaluated by a team of specialists to make sure the prospective transgender is psychologically stable and free of depression, anxiety, bi-polar, schizophrenia, dissociation or any personality disorder and does not have a history of suicide ideation or attempted suicide.

3. The best the gender surgery can do is make a person look different cosmetically.

You, the patient, must understand there are no guarantees that any amount of psychotherapy, intensive psychology testing, and group therapy will prevent suicide or regret. Just remember the surgeons can't change you from a male into a normal female--your body and the surgeons have limitations.

Even if you are delusional enough to believe you can change genders there is no guarantee during or after your transition that you will not commit suicide. Regret evolves after gender surgery. Even if at first you think you will benefit from the radical procedure, that feeling can fade in the face of real life and life will be no cupcake out there for transgenders over the long term.

The ripped-off transgender will be able to get a phony birth record. Regret and suicide risks will remain high as long as suicide prevention remains a side show.

See supporting evidence in other blog posts:
4/30/2013 Physician Says: "We have willfully failed"
5/6/2013 Transgenders, 4 Studies Say It's Mental Disorders

 Walt Heyer, the Maverick Transgender
www.sexchangeregret.com

In the next blog entry, the whistle-blowing physician reveals recent research which he thinks shows great promise in finding the actual cause of GID. What makes this very exciting to me is that having this knowledge should lead to the development of truly effective treatment to replace the current folly of gender surgeries, hormonal treatments, regret and suicide.

05/27/2013

Transitioning May Become Obsolete

I've heard again from the gender-insider physician who writes to tell me about a study published last week. I've italicized the words that I want to make sure you see.

Dear Walt, this just came out electronically ahead of print 1 week ago. It demonstrates that the main factor in the brain that is responsible for brain growth and changes of the brain in those with Gender Identity Disorder (GID):

1. Parallels the same brain neurochemistry and neurophysiology that is known to underpin various mental disorders in general

2. Is directly the result of the way transsexuals are treated mainly in traumas and psychological abuse

I can't pick and choose the objectivity of the facts. I now need to present you the objective findings that neurochemistry and the neurophysiology of GID brains demonstrates that the brain is indeed changeable and that there is substantial evidence that *GID brains are the result of psychological trauma* and that the changes are the changes seen in those with an array of psychiatric disorders. Read below —

Brain-derived neurotrophic factor (BDNF) plays a critical role in neurodevelopment and neuroplasticity. Altered BDNF-signaling is thought to contribute to the pathogenesis of *psychiatric disorders* and is related to traumatic life events...This data support the hypothesis that the reduction found in serum BDNF levels in GID patients may be related to the *psychological abuse that transsexuals are exposed during their life.*

Since BDNF is involved in neurophysiology and neurochemistry and is subject to change based on the environment, I am not confident that what seems to be a cross sexed brain structure actually is a cross sexed brain structure in any of the transsexual brain studies now or perhaps to come. It may be that transsexualism is not ever a male/female brain issue and raises the possibility that *neuropsychiatric treatment will substitute and replace gender surgeries and hormonal treatments for all transsexuals.* The authors went by the book and diagnosed the subjects according to the DSM criteria of GID. So they were not misdiagnosed. Even if 10-20% of transsexuals may benefit from treatment with transitioning, the transitions and SRS may become outmoded in favor of neurological and neuropsychiatric treatments. *This study may be the one which starts the revolution to show that transitioning is idealistically an obsolete treatment.*

This article is the biggest that I have ever seen on the brain in GID. I see it as a call to now look for neuropsychiatric treatments for transsexual and transgender conditions and for not only a phasing out of hormonal and SRS treatments but also a warning that technologies that may be developed that could eventually lead to a normal man becoming a normal woman or vice versa would not prevent regrets nor help the mental illness issues that this study has shown gender identity problems to be.
Ref: http://www.ncbi.nlm.nih.gov/pubmed/23702250

117

Neuropsychiatric treatments could make gender transitioning obsolete and could offer new treatment criteria. This gives me optimism that it may help reduce the needless surgeries and unnecessary suicides.

Walt Heyer, the Maverick Transgender
www.sexchangeregret.com

Recently, a person emailed me with a technical question about XO/XY mosaicism causing transgenderism:

Walt, most people who are trans have mental disorders. About the minority who don't, where can I find evidence that the XO/XY mosaicism is not the cause? Since the Y chromosome is absent in some of these cells (hence XO) it has been suggested that the transsexuals who need to align their body and will not ever regret it have this mosaicism. As you may know, XO cells since they have an absent (Y) chromosome do not replicate but disappear so it only looks like the person is normal XY when it was proved that they are XO/XY mosaics. Successes like Lynn Conway, Jenna Talackova, and so on. Please get me evidence that the mosaicism theory of the successful transsexual has been invalidated.

Thank goodness for the whistle-blowing physician who provided the answer:

Individuals who are XO/XY mosaics develop gender identity based upon healthy rearing. Even in intersexed individuals with very obvious XO/XY mosaicism even to the extent of causing mixed gonadal dysgenesis, the results show neither a brain effect nor the mosaicism indicates a gender identity.

118

Example: in a study by Zucker's group, all those with the condition reared as boys were happy and all with the condition reared as girls were happy.

Ref: http://www.ncbi.nlm.nih.gov/pubmed/18082854

Besides, it has been shown that the brain is NOT responsible for gender identity per se. Hormones and the brain could contribute to role behaviors like being more aggressive or doing a little better on verbal spatial tasks, but they do not cause gender identity. Healthy rearing, peer groups, and body image do.

Ref: http://link.springer.com/article/10.1023%2FB%3 AASEB.0000014324.25718.51

I have heard so many explanations of hypothetical physiological explanations for transsexualism and can say that there is no convincing evidence that there is a physiological basis for transsexualism. In fact, when intersexed people have the same identical condition and the same severity of that condition, the evidence always points to the fact that it is healthy rearing, self image and psychosocial forces that determine the child's gender identity.

My thanks go out to the whistle-blowing doctor whose help has been invaluable in addressing medical questions about gender issues.

Young lives and even the more mature lives are hanging in the balance. All that matters is that someone cares enough about transgender suicide to keep putting the information out there. I'll keep doing it as long as I have breath. These lives matter.

Families Are Suffering

12

The advocates do not give a damn about the pain-filled hearts
of mothers, fathers, siblings and spouses.
—*Walt Heyer, the maverick transgender*

Family members, including children, in mind-twisting bewilderment cannot grasp what drove their loved one to abandon their entire family, friends and their very birth gender. It is like they ran off to live in a gender cult where no real genders exist or are wanted.

When you start the process of changing of genders you feel like you have unintentionally stepped into sinking sand. This large pit of quicksand steadily sucks you in, ever downward and deeper. Sinking so deep into the transgender abyss, you become so fully involved there seems no light and no way out of the darkness. You lose touch with what is real. Reality fades as you slip into the marginalized and unknown twisted transgender world. You, and everyone who knows you, all start to wonder how this great person, even a smart person, stepped into this delusional, unyielding world of twisted genders. To onlookers, it looks like the cheese has slipped off the cracker for sure.

Unfortunately in our culture, we have universally embraced the lies that say you can change your gender. By embracing the lies we have greatly marginalized, suspended and given up on the truth. The truth is: it is medically, surgically and scientifically impossible to manufacture a female from a male or vice versa. Sure, you can surgically mutilate genitals on a man or add tissue to a woman to make genitalia that look like that of the opposite gender. That would be the surgically manufactured transgender sex gender.

The wives and families and beloved friends, are desperate to pull the transgender-to-be from the sinking sand. Most often we don't find out how entrenched they are until it is too late and they have fallen out of reach. We feel helpless. It looks like the quicksand will have a life-long hold on our loved one.

The entire transition is filled with mystery to the one undergoing it, but to onlookers it appears very self-centered and narcissistic, and in fact, it is. The delusional idea that ingesting heavy doses of hormones and undergoing multiple surgical procedures can change one's gender is pure fantasy. Living and acting in a gender persona you are not is pure Hollywood make-believe.

The transgender advocates envelope the gender changer in a cult-like way, closing the circle and keeping puzzled family and friends out. Transgenders have often been molested or experienced incest, family alcoholism, or drug-addicted parents—all issues known to directly cause psychiatric depressive issues. But parents are prevented from giving the approving psychologist information about childhood issues that need addressing.

Many good people, family and friends alike, are suffering because a loved one fell into the sinking sand of the transgender world. I want you to see the letters I receive and, if possible, try to hear their voices for they need to be heard. The letters will speak for themselves. The letters are shared with permission. Names and identifying details were deleted to protect their privacy.

First the wives—I want to show some of the pain and anger but also the compassion wives often have for a lost husband. This letter is an encouragement to me to keep writing and providing resources to those who are struggling.

Hello again Walt,

I wanted to let you know that I have read your book and it has been very beneficial to me.

I have so many emotions right now, and I have a much greater understanding of what my husband has been going through all these years; little by little I am putting pieces together from this puzzle.

I believe he had the surgery yesterday. I had been feeling a lot of anger and my own hurt for awhile and we had not spoken for a week; but God was preparing me to talk to him by filling my heart with love and compassion. I am sure, due in part to having read most of your book the day before.

I am trying not to think a lot about the future, and I am just taking one moment at a time. When I get thinking too much, I start reciting Bible verses in my mind, and it has been helping. I am so happy for you, and the wonderful way God has brought you through your journey, and especially bringing your wife into your life. My journey is far from over, but God has given me hope that perhaps we may still have a future together. We both always felt God had brought us together and that we were soul mates. My prayer is that God will be glorified in this somehow. He is being glorified through your struggle, and His faithfulness to you.

I will be sending for more copies of your book because there are a lot of people who will benefit from reading it.

In another letter we see the secrecy of a transgender hubby using hormones and not telling his wife—

I am a wife of a man that thinks that he's trapped inside of a woman's body. We've been married for 19 years and about a year and a half ago he told me he couldn't do this anymore that he needed to become a woman. We went to counseling that included me for about 2 sessions and then him on his own for 5 months. I was called back in to be told he was being referred to a GID [Gender Identity Disorder] counselor.

During the process of changing counselors I found out he had been taking hormones for just over a year before he told me. When I would ask about his body changing he would say it wasn't and that it was age or something.

Long story short—we have split up but he is questioning if there is something other than surgery that can help. He knows more than the doctors and it makes finding someone to talk to difficult because most feel the way of treatment is to allow the surgery. He wants me to accept this and be with a woman and I can't do that.

Please tell me if there is anyone out there that counsels instead of recommending surgery. I know God can do miracles and I'm looking for one but until then what? He wants to talk to someone that has beaten this. If you can help with resources or communicate with him please let me know. I want my husband and my children want their dad. I am desperate. Thank you for your time.

She says he wants to talk to someone who has beaten this, but when I offered to talk with him, he declined. He wants no help, except help to make the change. He would not talk to me. The hubby wants to appear to try but in truth is being deceptive.

Next, we see the ugly face of suicide thoughts. How is it they tell people "Go ahead—get a gender change" when this is the end result? From a wife of over twenty years—

I know that he is desperate for friendship and company, something that he avoided like the plague when we were married. I still love him and I pray for him and talk to him a little on the phone, but I CANNOT see him, it would crush me. In his latest e-mail he wrote that he thinks about driving off the road when he is on his motorcycle going 100-130 mph.

Do you have any thoughts for me? I know that I am the ex-wife, but I also believe that I am still the person that cares about him the most. I have put him in the Father's hands where I know he is safe, protected, provided for, comforted, guided and healed. I wish that I could be more there for him, but I know that it would finish breaking my heart if I saw him looking like a woman.

She was trying to get him into suicide counseling. We do not know the results, just the awful pain for her and him.

I try to stay up with people who contact me. This is from a mom who in her struggle says she is resting in God. She displays no scorn for her son, only comfort from a prayer team and faith in Christ—

Thank you for checking in with me. Although I am still struggling with turning my worries over to God, I have found a greater sense of peace in recent weeks. Speaking with you helped me to let go of the control I was searching for and to realize that the future is truly in God's hands.

This is not the first time I have watched my adult children make decisions that are not in line with their upbringing, but this is certainly the most serious in terms of potential for life-long repercussions.

I had a lengthy discussion with my pastor which proved to be an encouragement and reminder that we all have varying degrees of sin, but those are often what God uses to draw us to Him. I still pray that God will my son's hormone therapy and reassignment surgery, but most of all, I pray that He will bring him to salvation. There are many praying for him because he is blinded by it all and has no knowledge of the consequences on the road ahead of him.

This next note is from a woman who points out the growing role the internet has in shaping our young kids' minds, as she tells of the journey of a friend's daughter—

I know a very troubled young girl, who, at about age 13, saw a web site on F to M sex change and suddenly decided she had been born the wrong sex. THAT was the cause of all her problems--her social isolation, her obsessions and her continual conflict with her controlling mother. Her mother took her to a prominent sex change therapist in Boston who prescribed testosterone. She has just turned 18, was just hospitalized for anorexia, and is below the tenth percentile for females in height and weight.

Those few who can pull off the sex-change masquerade may fair well enough in their new roles but this poor girl is a grotesque caricature of a man. It is so sad. None of her problems have been solved. They have only gotten worse.

Best wishes

I shared these letters because I think it is important to provide a broader picture of the fall-out from this horrible barbaric surgery only Dr. Frankenstein would be applauding. To me, the whole practice of approving people who are truly in deep pain for surgery is appalling because the outcomes do not show sufficient success. Knife and hormones will never cure psychological issues or provide lasting relief from pain. It is so damn easy to see. I'm not wearing any special Superman eyewear. Thirty percent are dying from suicide. Do you need more proof the sex change is a failure? I sure don't.

A Shout Out for Sanity

13

It is more difficult to be approved for a home loan today
than gender sex changing surgery.
—Walt Heyer, the maverick transgender

One of the biggest misconceptions about gender surgery is that the individuals who gain approval have followed a step-by-step progression through rigorous requirements, but that is not the case. The key to the prevention of gender change regret and suicide rests on the knowledge and skill of the approving therapists, no one else.

Over the years I have thoughtfully taken every opportunity to show how much false and misleading information has come from the activists about the success of changing genders and how their claim that life as a transgender is always wonderful is sadly not the case. I continue to document on my blog and website facts that should make anyone skeptical about the gender surgery.

In this manuscript we have attempted to shine the light on the truth, exposing how the treatment procedure does not reduce the very high rate of suicide and suicide attempts. The suicides occur because the evaluation and diagnosing of gender dysphoria are done too quickly. The diagnosis is often arrived at casually, without any consideration for childhood abuse, perceived abandonment, family alcohol or psychiatric issues including family suicide history. So often, deeper issues exist.

Consider this: it is more difficult to be approved for a home loan today than gender sex changing surgery. The loan companies look into your background on several levels to see how sound and able you are. The opposite is true for the therapists approving transgenders for surgery. They will approve someone for surgery no matter what. The therapists claim that transgenders (the patients) push them into writing the approval letters. I guess the transgenders are bullying the spineless therapists into approving them.

I had the gender surgery and I want you to know what I have learned. I want to show the evidence and expose as much as possible the false and misleading information propagandized by the LGBT to advance their agenda. Anyone who does not support them is labeled a homophobe, bigot and transphobe. That's fine with me; the truth will win.

Have no doubts. Transgenders are not formed in the womb but evolve slowly from unresolved childhood family issues, unresolved psychological disorders and other overlooked secondary disorders the activist therapists refuse to acknowledge exist. I know from all the letters I get and also from my own life experience that the current method of diagnosing a transgender is so darn pathetic it qualifies as a joke. There has been no improvement made in diagnosing transgenders over the last thirty years. My own trip down that path led to my surgery 30 years ago and nothing has changed since then. I hear often from transgenders and their family members who tell the same sad story today. Today political correctness stymies scientific research.

I'm fortunate that when I considered suicide I was in the care of an outstanding psychologist who turned me over to another psychologist. Thankfully he prevented my suicide.

Just because there is a written document called the "Standards of Care" to guide diagnosis and treatment of transgenders doesn't mean the standards are followed. Medical practices that rely on transgenders for their livelihood are not going to turn people who want surgery away. In fact, quite the opposite: more diagnoses of transgenders mean more money, without any accountability for the outcomes.

I have learned that the activists with their agenda for political power and social change often suppress the truth.

I have come to learn no matter how factual and well-crafted research studies are some will dismiss them as if they don't exist.

I have told you the many problems. Now let's consider how we solve regret and suicide. In my opinion, gender surgery is never medically necessary, but if they insist, here is my suggestion of a way to structure it to reduce regret and suicide:

I would first require a full family history and evaluation that could include time with each family member as part of the work-up, then a minimum two years one-on-one psychotherapy with a Ph.D. who has a track record of treating coexisting disorders. Then it would be time for a required two years of group therapy in concert with the real life cross-gender test, and further evaluations using psychology and personality tests. A person must not have a history of depression or abusing drugs or alcohol. He or she must have a decent non-criminal report, demonstrate a successful work and social life, and have handled hormone therapy for a minimum of 2 years before the final approval of surgery. This is the minimum protocol treatment standard in my view.

Solutions to prevent regret and suicide must be found.

Who will come alongside me and stand shoulder-to-shoulder to push for better standards, improved evaluations and comprehensive research that result in effective care and treatment for the transgender population?

Who will stand with me against the influence of the very vocal LGBT who have not, and will not, support true treatment for a suicidal population?

I have found that most of those with a story to tell or information to share are reluctant to come forward. So it falls to me to be the whistleblower.

I have blown the whistle. It is now a call to action for all of us to take a stand, to be aware, save lives, reduce regret and to stop the 40 years of complete gender change madness.

A Personal Message to Transgenders

14

Transgenders who enter into a surgical gender transformation commit birth gender suicide 100% of the time. Thirty percent—those who lose their lives to suicide—will have no opportunity to return to redeem their lost gender but you do.

Gender suicide is the only one you can come back from. You can redeem your birth gender all for the asking if you have an unwavering desire to come back. Along with the redeeming of your birth gender you will redeem your dignity, health, happiness and relationships and you will see blessings and favor you never, ever, thought possible. Everything is returned back to you if you desire to redeem yourself. This I know is true—it is my testimony of life today.

I'm not talking about redeeming your old life—that life was a mess and far too painful. No, I'm talking about redeeming your birth gender—the one you took so much time to cover up under plastic surgery, hormones and all that other stuff.

To start the process of redeeming your birth gender, find a quiet place alone, where no one else will see you. Then shout out loud to the sky and acknowledge that the doctors who injected you with hormones and the surgeons with their knives did not have power to change your gender. It was all an elaborate masquerade that helped you cover the pain of the past, but no more.

You know you did not actually change. The theatrical cosmetic surgery made you look different but under it all it is still your heart pumping away, waiting for you to return and love the old you in a new life free of pain and sorrow.

Listen, I know this is not for everybody, no, not at all. In fact, most will reject this notion and I fully understand. Also, I know that the tug to live the transgender life will try to pull you back and you feel powerless against it. That is because most of us will attempt to redeem our birth gender on our own strength. No one person has that much strength or power. It takes more power than any of us have alone.

Many are addicted to the transgender life, no different than the heroin addict with a needle stuck in his arm, not living a real life at all, just an empty, pain-filled shell of a person looking for a way out. There is a way out but the catch is you've got to hit bottom and admit you were wrong. Perhaps you would have been better off at the very beginning fighting the poison but you drank it and succumbed.

If you want a better life, redeeming your gender is a good start. Not that old broken heartache life, but your original gender in a new life.

If you really want the jubilee life with healthy relationships, even with your family, like I have, then it is time to look at faith. It will be *your ticket out* so you can join the jubilee celebration. No doubt that well of poison will whisper out to you, calling you back to all the pain, sorrow, brokenness, and despair but that is no real life at all.

My own broken-down, sorry life started badly and did not stop quickly. I lost everything, my career, my kids and that was by far the most painful experience of my sorry life. Yes, I lost my marriage and my family. I lost most of my old relationships, the ones that connected my present with a life all gone now. They wanted nothing to do with me and I could not and did not blame them.

There is a reason your life got so twisted. Here is the story I wrote a few years ago about mine. For me the hurts started when I was young.

Only 8 years old—why was this happening to me? Night after night tears streamed down my little cheeks, soaking my pillow. I hated what was happening. How could I make Uncle Fred stop touching me? Mom didn't believe me when I told her about it; she said I was a liar. Was she just protecting him?

I formed a fantasy getaway in my head where no one could hurt me. I enjoyed visiting the secret place where I was safe from being hurt by Uncle Fred.

Tormented by the toxic shame of my nasty secret, I grew into a confused young man. The painful childhood memories would not go away. Marriage, children and a career—I thought they would help, but now the crying was internal. The inner conflict raged, ripping at my core identity.

I was so mixed up. I used alcohol and drugs. Soon a divorce followed and what "they" said was a mental disorder called Gender Identity Disorder. The "treatment" for this disorder cut away perfectly good body parts to fabricate a surgical female and a new identity. The boy surgically and legally destroyed, I finally turned to the Lord in a small church where Pastor Jeff said, "As your church family our job is to love you." And, oh, I so needed the Lord's love. That little church family prayed for me and my restoration almost every day for months. Then it was discovered I suffered from multiple personality disorder resulting from Uncle Fred's frequent sexual molestations. The surgical "treatment" had been a very destructive mistake.

During one counseling session that lasted nearly five hours, my Christian psychologist began to pray with me. My eyes closed, my head down, I could see so clearly the Lord reaching out for me. He was real; He spoke to me, "Come with me. You will be safe with me forever." The prayer was soon over but the Lord's healing power was just beginning.

My life today is filled to the brim with richness and joy. I'm completely restored as a man, husband, father and grandpa.

Today I pray for others as Pastor Jeff did for me in that little church so many years ago. I'm living proof of the Lord's grace, love and power to restore lives, no matter how broken.

You see, no matter how tough life is and how foolish we are at times, we can restore what was lost and make life better than ever. Your life will be better than you ever or anyone ever thought was possible, yes it will. That old poison that once looked so exciting, the one I drank for eight years, from that transgender well was slowly killing me. I was so close I almost died. I was at the edge so close, too close I started thinking about suicide I wanted to be dead.

I worked to make the life of Laura Jensen all it could be. In fact, I accomplished that, but that life was a transgender life. I knew there had to be more, much more to life than being a transgender female, because that sure is not much. A real life with real people had much more to offer and I could see that with my own eyes.

I wanted to redeem my birth gender, not my sorry old alcoholic, pain-filled life and mental disorders. No, I wanted to live life by faith. I chose faith in God as the way I wanted to live. I want you to know I'm not a religious person. I'm not in a religious church with all the rules the religious people love. That religion stuff is not for me; they can have it. But God—I want all I can get of God in my life.

I chose life by faith over life in a fantasy world. When I did reach out in faith to God I also found a new personal relationship with the Lord Jesus Christ. God provided me with a new well, his well of life to drink from. I continue to drink from that well today and I thirst no more.

To be redeemed we must first have faith in God.

Your new faith, if you choose faith, will please both you and God. First, please understand God cares enough for you to fill your desire to be restored to him. He is there no matter how broken you feel. He can put the pieces back and you will come to love Him. Anyone who wants joy will pursue a personal relationship with God and not settle for anything less.

You can have your transgender life. Be a transgender and remain attached to all that stuff you think is so much fun.

But you know in your heart your life is all broken up. When you are tired of the old life and want real joy, happiness and a new mended heart, you can embrace faith and ask God to help you stop drinking the poison in that old well.

The result of drinking poison is pain, depression and even suicide, because taking enough of that poison will eventually kill you.

All the studies in this book show a sex change is filled with heartache, sickness, pain, living in poverty or ending in suicide. Now that is a poison well but you do not need that well and can have a much better life than you ever dreamed possible.

You can, if you want, stop hurting your family and others, sucking on an empty baby bottle of empty promises and empty dreams. It's your choice. I'm glad I let go of the man from hell. He can go die without me.

Sucking down the transgender poison is killing you. You can instead do what I did.

Today my life is fabulous because I turned to Jesus. I removed myself from a life that was poisoning me. Now I'm free from the old disorders.

You can enjoy the jubilee where everything of true value that was lost is given back to you: everything your bad choices took from you or you threw away by how you lived your masquerade life. You still have to live with the physical scars from all those surgeries but you'll get back everything that matters.

Let me illustrate how turning to God led to a new life for me by sharing some of my story.

Through friends at church I met Kaycee. She was fourteen years younger than me and traveled all over the world in her work. I, on the other hand, had come through some very tough times—alcoholism and mental illness—and worked from job to job without much direction. So I knew there was no possibility of a love interest developing between us. When she asked me to take the Myers-Briggs personality profile test for the fun of it, I kidded her, telling her: "I have no personality." She reviewed her list of 35 personality traits she wanted in a soul-mate and was surprised that I had 34 that matched. Embarrassed, I said, "I have a list, too." When she replied, "I know what's on your list. You just want to make sure she's breathing!" we laughed with gusto. Was love at work here? I wondered. "We're friends—that's all," she insisted.

I invited her to a movie. Sitting next to her I had this incredible urge to hold her hand. Like a little kid, slowly I inched my hand toward hers. I waited until I got the nerve, then gently placed my hand on hers. Oh, oh, oh, the electricity, the chemistry! My past or her youth, it did not matter; this was the feeling of love and remarkably, she allowed my hand to stay on hers.

I was falling in love, but what about her? One day I asked if we could wash her red convertible and then go to a park just to sit and talk. We got to the park and walked across the grass to a bench, where I felt my heart race as I gasped and told her I loved her. She had this funny look on her face; when I started to walk away, over my shoulder I heard her say: "I love you, too." I jumped into the air with joy.

Love overcomes all. When I thought life had gotten the best of me and figured that no one could ever love me, along came one who only saw my heart, not my scarred life and uneven past. They say love is blind, but my experience is that unconditional love inspires us to be *our best. And through these years of marriage to Kaycee, that awesome power called love has transformed and healed us both. That's the story of love.*

The jumping in the air with joy is the Lord's gift of a restored birth gender; not the old life of pain but a life of jubilee celebration. Kaycee and I still jump in the air with joy because the jubilee celebration continues, even now after over sixteen years of marriage.

I share this chapter with you as an inspiration for you to have the faith in God. He will also bring you into a jubilee celebration of life, if you ask him. Now it is time for your own personal journey to sanity and a new life in Jesus Christ.

Glossary

DSM: Diagnostic and Statistical Manual of Mental Disorders
The tool most widely referenced by clinicians in the mental health field, published since 1952 by The American Psychiatric Association and now in its fifth revision, also known as DSM-5.

LGBT: Lesbian, Gay, Bi-sexual, Transgender
May also be written GLBT or LGBTQ for Questioning or Queer

Standards of Care; WPATH Standards of Care
Full name is "Standards of Care for the Health of Transsexual, Transgender, and Gender Nonconforming People"
The goal of the SOC is "to provide clinical guidance for health professionals to assist transsexual, transgender, and gender nonconforming people with safe and effective pathways to achieving lasting personal comfort with their gendered selves..." (www.wpath.org)
Originally called the Harry Benjamin Standards of Care

WPATH: The World Professional Association for Transgender Health
A professional organization devoted to the understanding and treatment of gender identity disorders. (www.wpath.org)
Formerly known as the Harry Benjamin International Gender Dysphoria Association (HBIGDA)

Online Sources of Information

www.WaltHeyer.com
www.SexChangeRegret.com
www.TradingMySorrows.com

Contact the Author

waltsbook@yahoo.com

More Books *by* Walt Heyer

Paper Genders

Pulling the Mask off
the Transgender Phenomenon

A fresh perspective on treatment
of gender identity issues.

Well-researched, yet personal.

"The research, reason, passion and
compassion makes for compelling
reading."

Paper Genders

Il Mito del Cambiamento di Sesso

Italian translation
SUGARCO Edizion

Prefazione di Italo Carta

Con un saggio de
R. P. Fitzgibbons,
P. M. Sutton, D. O'Leary

More Books *by* Walt Heyer

Trading My Sorrows

A true story of betrayals, bad choices, love and the journey home

"Walt's story...a true miracle story ...about a very personal and powerful struggle..."

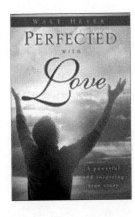

Perfected with Love

"A powerful and inspiring true story..." that teaches of the radical nature of love in action.

Available online at www.sexchangeinfo.com and amazon.com.